The Arch Street Ferry *in Philadelphia was engraved by William and Thomas Birch*.

COVER: *This 1799 painting by Francis Guy of the corner of Wall and Water Streets shows the Tontine Coffee House (left), which housed the Stock Exchange.*

FRONT ENDSHEET: *Washington reviews troops called to put down the Whiskey Rebellion in 1794, when Pennsylvania farmers rioted over a tax on liquor.*

CONTENTS PAGE: *American naval uniforms were dressier in 1812 than today.*

BACK ENDSHEET: *The Battle of New Orleans, as drawn on the field by an American army engineer, was fought two weeks after peace was signed. The British lost more than 2,000, including three generals. The Americans lost only 71.*

*"A knowledge of the past prepares us for the crisis
of the present and the challenge of the future."*

JOHN F. KENNEDY
From his special foreword in Volume 1

THE AMERICAN HERITAGE
NEW ILLUSTRATED HISTORY
OF THE UNITED STATES

VOLUME 4

A NEW NATION

By ROBERT G. ATHEARN
Professor of History, University of Colorado

CREATED AND DESIGNED BY THE EDITORS OF
AMERICAN HERITAGE
The Magazine of History

PUBLISHED BY
DELL PUBLISHING CO., INC., NEW YORK

CONTENTS OF THE COMPLETE SERIES

Foreword by JOHN F. KENNEDY
Introduction by ALLAN NEVINS
Main text by ROBERT G. ATHEARN

Vol. 1   THE NEW WORLD
Special picture portfolios:
THE SPANISH CONQUEST
THE PILGRIMS' EUROPE
Special contributor:
THOMAS F. McGANN—
THE ORDEAL OF CABEZA DE VACA

Vol. 2   COLONIAL AMERICA
Special picture portfolios:
THE FRENCH AND INDIAN WARS
LIFE IN COLONIAL AMERICA
Special contributor:
A. L. ROWSE—
THE PILGRIM AND PURITAN FATHERS

Vol. 3   THE REVOLUTION
Special picture portfolios:
THE DECLARATION OF INDEPENDENCE
THE ARMS AND THE MEN
Special contributor:
GEORGE F. SCHEER—
FRANCIS MARION: THE ELUSIVE SWAMP FOX

Vol. 4   A NEW NATION
Special picture portfolios:
THOMAS JEFFERSON
THE WAR AT SEA
Special contributor:
OLIVER JENSEN—
THE MANY-FACETED MR. PEALE

Vol. 5   YOUNG AMERICA
Special picture portfolios:
STIRRINGS OF INDUSTRY
NEW ROADS—THE WATERWAYS
Special contributor:
ARNOLD WHITRIDGE—
ELI WHITNEY: NEMESIS OF THE SOUTH

Vol. 6   THE FRONTIER
Special picture portfolios:
THE GREAT GOLD RUSH
INDIANS OF THE PLAINS
Special contributor:
STEPHEN W. SEARS—JEDEDIAH S. SMITH:
UNSUNG PATHFINDER OF THE WEST

Vol. 7   WAR WITH MEXICO
Special picture portfolios:
WAR IN THE WEST
WHALERS AND CLIPPERS
Special contributor:
GERALD W. JOHNSON—
DANIEL WEBSTER: GREAT MAN ELOQUENT

Vol. 8   THE CIVIL WAR
Special picture portfolios:
PRESIDENT LINCOLN
THE NAVAL WAR
Special contributor:
BRUCE CATTON—"HAYFOOT, STRAWFOOT!"

Vol. 9   WINNING THE WEST
Special picture portfolios:
COWBOYS—LIFE ON THE RANGE
THE LAST WARS WITH THE INDIANS
Special contributor:
STEWART H. HOLBROOK—
THE LEGEND OF JIM HILL

Vol. 10   AGE OF STEEL
Special picture portfolios:
MAKE WAY FOR THE IRON HORSE!
THE ROBBER BARONS
Special contributor:
JOHN A. GARRATY—
WILLIAM JENNINGS BRYAN

Vol. 11   THE GILDED AGE
Special picture portfolios:
THE ROMANTIC WORLD OF CURRIER AND IVES
THE VICTORIAN LOOK
Special contributor:
NELSON LANSDALE—
MRS. GARDNER AND HER PALACE

Vol. 12   A WORLD POWER
Special picture portfolios:
THE SPANISH-AMERICAN WAR
THE CITY GOES MODERN
Special contributor:
ROBERT L. HEILBRONER—
ANDREW CARNEGIE: EPITAPH FOR THE STEELMASTER

Vol. 13   WORLD WAR I AND THE TWENTIES
Special picture portfolios:
THE WAR IN THE AIR
AMERICA AS ADVERTISED
Special contributor:
ALLAN NEVINS—
HENRY FORD: A COMPLEX MAN

Vol. 14   THE ROOSEVELT ERA
Special picture portfolios:
F.D.R.
THE ARTIST'S AMERICA
Special contributor:
MERLO J. PUSEY—
F.D.R. VS. THE SUPREME COURT

Vol. 15   WORLD WAR II
Special picture portfolios:
D-DAY
THE UNITED NATIONS
Special contribution:
ONE WHO SURVIVED:
THE NARRATIVE OF ALLEN HEYN

Vol. 16   AMERICA TODAY
Special picture portfolio:
THE WORLD OF OUTER SPACE
The Presidents and the Presidential elections
The Presidents and their cabinets
Index of the complete series

A MASTER INDEX FOR ALL 16 VOLUMES APPEARS IN VOLUME 16

CONTENTS OF VOLUME 4

Chapter 10. MEN AND OPPORTUNITY   274

Chapter 11. WASHINGTON AT THE HELM   300

Chapter 12. THE REPUBLICAN ERA   332

SPECIAL PICTURE PORTFOLIOS:

        Thomas Jefferson   291

        The War at Sea   317

SPECIAL CONTRIBUTOR:

        OLIVER JENSEN

        The Many-Faceted Mr. Peale   350

No I.

[SATURDAY, OCTOBER 27, 1787.]

THE

INDEPENDENT JOURNAL:

[NUMBER 408.]

OR, THE

GENERAL ADVERTISER.

NEW-YORK: PUBLISHED EVERY WEDNESDAY
PRINTING-OFFICE, N

FEDERALIST.

I.

Geo Robt. an
Lewis

JOHNSON'S DICTIONARY

COMMON PRAYER

KEN DAVIS

CHAPTER 10

Men and opportunity

It is a difficult thing to see one age through the eyes of another, to hear with it, feel with it, think with it, and to grasp the spirit of other times. Yet those who study the record of the American Revolution and the years immediately following it cannot escape the conclusion that this was, for all its struggle, one of the great periods of history in which to be alive.

To the former colonists themselves —and even more so to Europeans—it was astonishing that in seven years they could actually achieve the life and liberty they had proclaimed. Would they now also succeed in that even more difficult quest—the "pursuit of happiness"?

The 18th century, that era of enlightenment which liked to call itself the Age of Reason, looked hopefully to the American Republic. Europe had come to know the eminent Dr. Franklin—scientist, wit, philosopher, and democrat; if the other Americans were like him, then the future of his country was promising. Perhaps the

Portraits of Madison, Jay, and Hamilton surround manuscript, newspaper, and book copies of the Federalist essays they wrote.

New World would at last achieve and make into law the "rights of man" about which men had argued so long. These sturdy farmers called to mind the Romans in the days of the Republic. Unlike jaded Europe, they had no mob, no nobles, no king. Indeed, their great General Washington, like Cincinnatus 2,000 years before, had laid down his sword, bowed to the Congress, and returned to his farm, a hero out of Plutarch.

This was, perhaps, a sentimental picture, but it was true that the leaders of America had classic models, Greek and Roman, before their eyes as they set to organizing their new life as freemen. They were, unlike so many revolutionists before and afterward, well-educated and open-minded believers in "natural law"—a kind of common-sense set of universal rules made by the Creator, under which men had innate title to civil liberties, to popular sovereignty, and to the right of revolt. They owed, they felt, nothing to the past, which Washington called "a gloomy age of ignorance and superstition."

The war had brought forward many talented men, and now these same young public figures, uplifted by the sense that they lived in a climactic moment of history, proved themselves great. Alexander Hamilton, Thomas Jefferson, James Madison, John Marshall, John Adams, John Dickinson, George Mason, and a dozen more—these Founding Fathers stare down at us stiffly like old men in their formal portraits, all ruffles and high collars and powdered wigs, but they were very much alive in those days. Never has a young nation been so richly endowed with vigorous leaders.

A raw new country

Nor has a country been so in need of them. Excepting only the uncounted Indians, scarcely 3,000,000 people lived in the new states, and all but a handful of them lived in the country. Philadelphia, the largest city, had 40,000 inhabitants. New York had 30,000, Boston 20,000. Most people clung to the seaboard, or lived near tidewater on which they could travel and ship their goods, for roads were primitive and slow. Even between Boston and New York, served by a stagecoach three times a week, the trip took three jogging, bouncing, uncomfortable days. It was two more days to Philadelphia. In the South there were no roads or stages at all, and the traveler went on horseback, following paths and trails. Of necessity, the states lived separate and apart on the civilized edge of a continent no one had crossed. Behind the coastal fringe lay the still-untamed Alleghenies, and

beyond them a few frontier settlements dotted the vast Northwest Territory, today's Middle West, which the United States had acquired from England in the peace settlement.

The vast majority of the people lived by a primitive agriculture. There were no factories, for the Industrial Revolution still lay in the future. Almost all the necessities of life were made at home, and the typical farmer supported his family by means and methods that had seen little change in a thousand years. The only power was supplied by animals, wind and water, and human muscle. It was a hard, if often rewarding, life, and even then not all the 3,000,000 quite lived up to the hopeful visions of the faraway philosophers in Paris: Six hundred thousand of the Americans were Negro slaves, most but not all in the South. Three hundred thousand of the white men were not free either, but bound to service for some period of time as indentured servants, in payment of their passage to America. Of the rest, fully half were women who had no voting rights, and even among the freemen who made up the balance, perhaps only about 120,000 could meet all the property, religious, and other requirements for the franchise in the several states. Although the United States was a middle-class nation and had general social democracy as it began its experiment with political liberty, it was neither united nor democratic in its government, and it had need of all the brilliance that

The first American map of the United States, by Adam Buell in 1784, extends Connecticut, Virginia, the Carolinas, Georgia, Florida to the Mississippi.

the Founding Fathers could bring to bear on its many problems.

If the best government is the least government, as many philosophers have contended, the United States in 1783 had the world's finest. Certainly it had the least government of any civilized country. During the long

277

war, the Continental Congress had, of course, done all within its power to manage the fighting and carry on a government. It had contracted offensive and defensive alliances, raised an army, tried to establish a navy, borrowed money, and issued currency, however unstable that currency turned out to be. Its only authority was necessity, and its few commands, therefore, had been generally accepted.

A formal instrument of government had indeed been proposed in 1776, by the same Richard Henry Lee who had offered the resolution for independence. His Articles of Confederation were adopted in 1777, but did not come into effect—fortunately, perhaps—until 1781, when the war was all but over. For they weakened even further the power of the central government, which, as Washington observed in dismay, was "a half-starved, limping" thing, unable to govern or restrain the states. The Congress, said Dr. Benjamin Rush of Philadelphia, was "abused, laughed at, and cursed in every company." In fact, in June, 1783, when a group of disgruntled and threatening veterans marched on Philadelphia to demand their back pay, Congress had to flee to Princeton, New Jersey, penniless and abject. Was poor old George III so wrong when he observed more in sorrow than in anger that the United States "certainly for many years cannot have any stable government"?

Family quarrels

Even before the war was safely won, there were enough squabbles among the states to suggest that the king might be right. One state, for example, would arouse the animosity of the others by refusing to obey the requisitions of Congress. Neighboring states would battle over boundaries,

and there were countless arguments about trade regulations. Such wrangling not only embarrassed the central government, but was unnecessarily hard on foreign commercial houses. European nations naturally shied away from trade treaties with a country so weak and divided. From the outset, the credit rating of the United States was poor.

Rivalry was intense among the major seaports. In the lower South, most imports entered at Charleston; in the upper South, at Baltimore. The middle states received their foreign goods at either Philadelphia or New York, and New England at Boston. Immediately after the war, most of the states placed revenue-raising tariffs on imports. New England and the middle states, in particular, were developing home industries, and here tariffs were intended to protect them. The South, having no promising manufacturing, held its rates low, hoping to keep down the prices of goods its people bought. Southerners fumed at New England as a result.

On their part, the small New England states were bitter about the money New York made by virtue of its superior port facilities. Many of the articles used in Connecticut, New Jersey, Vermont, and western Massachusetts were bought in New York. Tariff revenues were of course added to the price. Unhappy residents of Connecticut claimed they paid an annual toll of 50,000 pounds into the New York treasury. New Jersey merchants were especially unhappy over the situation, and called for some centralized government power that would protect the little states. Matters got even worse when in 1787 the New York legislature decided to collect entrance and clearance fees from vessels trading with such foreign lands as New Jersey and Connecticut.

The 13 independent Americas

Because the states were long used to trading with the British, they naturally tried to continue. In 1785, John

When the Massachusetts legislature refused to aid the farmers, they rebelled in 1786 under Daniel Shays, attacking officials and the Springfield arsenal.

Adams went to London as the first official American minister, seeking to re-establish a healthy commerce. The king received him politely, but the British foreign minister was not quite so agreeable. Adams was advised that if the United States wished to make a trade treaty, *they* ought properly to, send over 13 representatives, as there was no sign of unity at home.

In the eyes of the British, our new government was guilty of a kind of bad faith, for Congress could not persuade the quarreling states even to live up to the peace treaty signed by their representatives. In it, America had promised creditors on each side that they would not be prevented from collecting their lawful debts at full sterling value. It had also agreed to urge upon the state legislatures the necessity of returning confiscated estates taken from British subjects. Loyalists who had fought for England, many of them now penniless and desperate, were to be granted a full year to go anywhere in the United States and press for the return of their property. The treaty had further stated there would be no more confiscations.

When the states learned that Congress had made such promises, they objected vigorously. Nevertheless, in January, 1784, Congress issued a proclamation asking all states holding property taken from the loyalists to return it. Fearing unrest and possibly riots if they tried to carry out the request, the state legislatures did not hurry to comply. It is not one of the brightest pages in our history. In almost every state there were violations of the Treaty of 1783. Southerners were more inclined than Northerners to ignore Congress, for the British had carried off or freed many Negro slaves without bothering to pay.

Time would heal the raw wounds of war, and the day would come when America's pledged word would be accepted, but the British were in no mood to wait for history; few creditors are. They applied pressure. By 1785, two years after the peace terms were signed, the United States learned that the British had no intention of evacuating their garrisons at Oswego, Niagara, Detroit, and other places until such offenders as New York and Virginia repealed some of their antiloyalist legislation. Even though men like Alexander Hamilton, George Washington, James Monroe, and John Marshall threw all their personal influence into the fight for compliance to treaty terms from their states, they were rebuffed, and the reputation of the Confederation government sank to a new low. Separatists were thriving, and a State of Franklin was actually set up, from 1784 to 1788, in western North Carolina. The Northwest was slipping away. Debts were mounting. Would the Confederation hold together?

Demands for a change

By 1787, Congress had failed so consistently to govern that it was held in almost no respect. Since the Revo-

When the Constitutional Convention, under Washington's leadership, met on May 25, 1787, at Independence Hall, the assemblage included most of the important American political leaders of the day.

lution, the quality of its membership had declined as each state persuaded its ablest leaders to stay in local positions.

So low had the interest in Congress sunk that that body could not even get the necessary quorum of nine states. From October, 1785, until April, 1786, there were only three days when enough members were present to conduct business. There was no money to pay civil officials or soldiers, and soldiers had mutinied. Money borrowed from Europe was exhausted, and American representatives abroad could not collect their salaries. There was ominous talk of establishing a monarchy, and many who abhorred the idea were forced to conclude that it was the only defense against chaos. George Washington saw that some drastic step was necessary when he wrote, "I do not conceive we can exist long as a nation without having lodged somewhere a power, which will pervade the whole Union in as energetic a manner as the authority of the State government extends over the several States."

Other thinking men also decided it was time for a change. As early as 1780, Alexander Hamilton, then only 23, declared that if Congress did not assume dictatorial powers, a general convention should be called. At his urging, the New York legislature later proposed such a meeting to amend the Articles of Confederation.

In 1785, Governor James Bowdoin of Massachusetts tried to hasten the movement for stronger central government when he recommended to his legislature the necessity of a convention. The legislators responded by asking Congress to call the states together. Unhappily, the course of state sovereignty was running at flood tide, and the Massachusetts delegates in Congress took it upon themselves to withhold the request. They asked the governor if this was not too bold a move. Perhaps they agreed with Jef-

ferson, then far away as the American minister at Paris, who wrote that he liked "a little rebellion now and then" and who wondered if the Indians, who had no central government at all, were not the best off.

By 1786, the independent spirit was running rampant throughout the states. In New Hampshire, mobs demanding a distribution of property and paper money rioted outside the building while legislators met. Rhode Island merchants were so hard-pressed by a law obliging them to accept payment in scrip that they closed their shops. Nearby, in Massachusetts, there was a frightening farmers' uprising. By 1785, their state taxes had risen to about a third of their income, which had to be paid in specie—hard money —something rarely seen on a farm. In 1786, taxes were raised again, the legislature refused to print cheap paper money, and debt-ridden farmers began to be evicted from their property by the courts. Daniel Shays, once a captain in the Revolution, and a band of 500 desperate men forced one court to close after facing down the state militia. Later, leading 1,200 men, he tried to seize the arsenal at Springfield and was routed only by gunfire.

It was a commercial question that finally prompted action. Maryland and Virginia fell to bickering over navigational rights on the Potomac

River, but agreed to discussion at Washington's Mount Vernon home. So successful were the talks that when Maryland suggested enlarging the agreements, the idea met with favor. Both Pennsylvania and Delaware showed interest, as did men like Hamilton and Madison, who had already been hard at work on proposed government reforms, and they took the necessary step of inviting all the states to a general trade convention. The meeting was arranged for September, 1786; the place, Annapolis. Although only five states actually sent delegates, Alexander Hamilton, representing New York and eager to use almost any device to strengthen the national government, managed to arrange another meeting—an all-important one as it turned out—at Philadelphia in May, 1787. James Madison assisted him. Congress cooperated by issuing the call, but specified that the meeting was to be for the sole purpose of revising the Articles of Confederation.

Hidden strengths of the Confederation

Although it unconsciously signed its own death warrant by agreeing to the Philadelphia convention, the old Confederation could nevertheless look back on a few achievements. During its later years, which historian John Fiske called the "critical period," it had provided the new nation with a greater sense of direction than many realized. Legend has it that Fisher Ames, soon to be a Congressman from Massachusetts, provided a pop-

At the Constitutional Convention, Edmund Randolph proposed the controversial Virginia Plan.

ular description of this new democracy. Monarchy, he said, is like a full-rigged ship, trim and beautiful, with all hands at their stations and the captain at the helm. It executes its maneuvers sharply and operates with the greatest efficiency, but if it hits a rock, the frail hull is crushed and the vessel sinks. Democracy is like a raft—hard to navigate, impossible to keep on course, and distressingly slow. If it runs onto a rock, it simply careens off and takes a new course. But if it has the virtue of always staying afloat, it has disadvantages, too. As Ames said, "Damn it, your feet are wet all the time."

Men who were distressed over the weakness of the Confederation government were more worried about wet feet than about the progress they had made, unnoticed. During its short history that government had formulated two of the most vital pieces of legislation in the history of the United States. The first was the farseeing Ordinance of 1785, which set forth the fundamentals of our land system and provided a pattern for the future.

This thoughtful law provided for a survey of Western lands, the property of the central government, into rectangular townships of 36 square miles each. Each square mile was called a section, and it contained 640 acres, sold for $1 each. By means of the advance survey, the government was able to mark off its salable land on maps and issue titles with more efficiency and equity. Although many sections fell into the hands of speculators and land companies, the survey still leaves its mark. Anyone flying across the nation today can observe the checkerboard result. Evidence that the young government was interested in education may be found in the fact that one section in every township was reserved for schools.

The Northwest Ordinance of 1787, the Confederation's second great piece of legislation, provided for the political subdivision of the territory north and west of the Ohio River known as the Northwest Territory. Slavery was to be excluded. By that law, a governor, a secretary, and three judges were appointed. When any of the territories laid out in that area contained 5,000 adult males, the people were to have a two-chamber legislature and a voice in their own government. When its free inhabitants reached 60,000, a territory might apply for statehood and attain equal standing with the other states. This was the direct opposite of the old European system; the states would have no colonies and only equal sisters. Daniel Webster later said that he doubted "whether one single law of any lawgiver, ancient or modern, has produced effects of more distinct, marked, and lasting character than the Ordinance of 1787."

Drawing up a new set of rules

The convention date had been set for May 14, 1787, but bad weather and worse roads delayed the arrival of a number of delegates. On May 25, a quorum of seven states was finally on hand. (New Hampshire was the last to arrive—over two months late—and Rhode Island never sent representatives at all.) Once the sessions began— at the old Pennsylvania State House, later known as Independence Hall with George Washington presiding— problems were attacked in earnest. To insure quiet in that era of cobblestones and noisy iron-rimmed wagon wheels, the streets in front of the building were muffled by spreading loose dirt. Public interest was great. Well-known figures like James Madison and Edmund Randolph of Virginia, Gouverneur Morris and Benjamin Franklin of Pennsylvania, and Rufus King of Massachusetts gathered at the sessions, and in off hours at the Indian Queen Tavern, to lend their talents to the work. The delegates ranged in age from Dr. Franklin, who was 81, to Jonathan Dayton of New Jersey, who was only 26. Jefferson, who was not present, was so impressed by their qualities that he referred to the meeting as "an assembly of demigods."

The leaders among the 55 delegates were ready for a bold step. They decided to ignore the instructions that they do nothing but amend the Articles of Confederation. Although the Confederation Congress was sitting nearby, working out the measures of the Northwest Ordinance, they resolved to devise a new form of government. To keep their proceedings secret, they posted sentries at the doors. For the same reason, few records were kept, and we owe our knowledge of the debates mainly to notes kept by James Madison, which were not published until more than half a century later, four years after his death.

At the start, Edmund Randolph of Virginia stepped forward with a plan named after his state. It proposed a two-house national legislature with the power to do all those things with respect to taxation, commerce, finance, war, and treaty making in which the old system had proved itself so weak. Under the Virginia Plan, the lower house would be elected by the people, and the upper house would be chosen by the lower from nominees of the state legislatures. The Virginians could observe, along with the new state governments, the English Parliament with its House of Lords and its House of Commons acting as a check upon each other—the hereditary Lords conservative and free from fickle popular favor, and the elected Commons (for all its faults in that era) the more representative voice of the people, with, in effect, the power to give money to the executive or withhold it from him. Randolph's plan also proposed an executive chosen by the legislature, a judiciary including a supreme court and lower courts, and a council of revision made up of the executive and several members of the judiciary with a veto power over the legislature.

There was much opposition to one point or another of the Virginia Plan, but most of it was centered around the fact that both houses of the legislature would be chosen on a basis of population. The small states were displeased because this meant they would have much less power than their heavily populated neighbors like Virginia and New York. And so the Virginia Plan was countered by a New Jersey Plan, representing the views of the small states. It returned to the idea of a single legislature, with one vote for every state, a plural executive with less power, and a supreme court. In essence it was the Articles of Confederation again, but with much greater power given to Congress. It also proposed to levy taxes on a basis proportionate to population, counting the whites in full and taking Negroes at three-fifths—a device that eventually

George Mason (left), a delegate to the Constitutional Convention from Virginia, and Elbridge Gerry (center) from Massachusetts refused to sign its final document. William Paterson countered the Virginia Plan with the New Jersey Plan.

carried over into the Constitution.

The argument was solved at last, as most are, by a compromise. Roger Sherman of Connecticut proposed that membership in the lower house be allotted in proportion to population, but that each state be equal in the other house, with one vote. The proposal was modified in the great debate that followed, but Sherman's suggestion paved the way to agreement and gave the country the House and Senate as they exist today.

When they came to provide an executive, the delegates turned away after a while from the notion of having this person (or persons) elected by Congress; they believed that dependence on the favor of an all-powerful legislature would weaken him too much. Only a few favored popular election—among them Dr. Franklin, John Dickinson, Gouverneur Morris,

and James Wilson. But most delegates felt that the people were simply not up to such a responsibility. They were not "sufficiently informed," thought Roger Sherman. Asking the people to pick a good executive was like referring "a trial of colors to a blind man," remarked George Mason.

The eventual compromise on this question was the work of Morris and Madison, who put forward an adaptation of the method used by Maryland in choosing its state senators—a body of electors. Each of the states, they suggested, would have as many electors as it had Representatives and Senators in Congress, appointed "in such manner as the legislature thereof may direct." This was indirect election. When the "electoral college" then voted for a President, it would elect the candidate who received a majority of the votes of all the electors. The

REDEUNT SATURNIA REGNA.

On the erection of the Eleventh PILLAR of the great National DOME, we beg leave most sincerely to felicitate " OUR DEAR COUNTRY."

Rise it will.

The foundation good—it may yet be SAVED.

The FEDERAL EDIFICE.

When the 11th state—powerful New York—ratified, the Constitution was considered nationally acceptable, even without North Carolina and Rhode Island.

runner-up would be Vice-President (although this was altered later). Even that leading conservative Alexander Hamilton, who had hoped for a lifetime executive, or "Governor," of the United States (with power to appoint state governors!), was satisfied with this solution. He was sure it would prevent any "cabal, intrigue, and corruption." Everyone assumed that the electors under this system would be the cream of American society, fiercely independent, pledged to no one person, and that they would consider long and carefully, often weighing many candidates, before choosing one to fill four years in the exalted office. What in fact has happened to the electoral college is well known, but it was not foreseen at that time. And as the delegates had that model of honor and rectitude, General Washington, in mind for the first President, they agreed to the electoral plan.

The one fact that stands out clearly in a document referred to as a "bundle of compromises" is the notion of the separation of powers. The states delegated some and kept others. Each of the three branches of the central government—legislative, executive, and judicial—was provided with the power to check the others. Congress could exercise a measure of control over the judiciary through its appointive power. The executive could veto an act of Congress, but that body in turn could override the veto. And, finally, the Supreme Court might declare unauthorized acts of Congress unconstitutional. As became apparent later, the most important question not answered was whether a state might withdraw—that is, secede—from the new Union.

When enough compromises had been made to reassure the delegates who were most fearful, the document was ready for signing. Then it came out that all the repairing and patching had produced a result unsatisfactory to other members. George Mason, Elbridge Gerry, and Edmund Randolph flatly refused to sign. Washington, Franklin, and Hamilton had reservations but, feeling that progress had been made, gave their approval. A man living in Philadelphia at the time of the convention later said that talks with various delegates had convinced him that no one of them was wholly satisfied.

Those who gathered at Philadelphia that summer of 1787 accomplished much more than they realized. Casting aside the relatively weak Articles of Confederation, whose only strength was based upon the willingness of individual states to cooperate, they forged a new instrument of great potential power. Inherent in the Constitution was the notion that sovereignty lay with individuals, not with state governments. The idea of democratic republics was not new, but in the European models, the component parts (or political subdivisions) contributed the power. In the new American Republic, both the states and the central government drew their authority from the same source—the people. And the people were citizens both of their home states and of the nation. By their actions the framers of the Constitution spread the national government's jurisdiction across the face of the nation, and for the first time made it possible for voters to decide upon purely national issues. They may not have regarded their work as revolutionary, as most of their ideas were drawn from earlier colonial experience, but the long-range result was to be far from conservative in its nature. As Madison commented, they had "built for the ages," and it was true. No other nation in the modern world is still governed by so ancient and durable an instrument. Yet, ironically enough, it would probably never have been adopted if there could, in that era, have been a popular vote.

The campaign for ratification

Although still having some doubts about the nature of their work, the delegates bravely presented it to their fellow Americans for approval. Trying to cover up their own disagreements, they said at the end of the Constitution that it was "done in convention by the unanimous consent of the states present," and the approval of ratifying conventions in nine states was required to make it binding. Pennsylvania at once called a convention, but it was beaten by Delaware. The little state, eager to benefit by the guarantees offered, became the first to ratify, in early December. A few days later another small state, New Jersey, went along. In January, 1788, Georgia and Connecticut followed. Not all of the smaller states were so enthusiastic. Rhode Island stood aloof and stoutly refused to join her sisters. Proponents of the new government were of course discouraged by this attitude, but then the important state of Massachusetts voted yes, 187 to 168. Although the Massachusetts majority was small, six states had now approved.

During the spring of 1788, victory for the Constitution makers was assured. Maryland and South Carolina ratified in April, New Hampshire and Virginia in June. The contest in Virginia was particularly violent, with the fiery Patrick Henry and the well-known Richard Henry Lee leading the opposition. They feared the loss of state power to the young giant spawned at Philadelphia. Only the persuasive powers of respected figures like Washington, Madison, and Marshall tipped the scales against them.

In New York the battle was no less spectacular. The seaboard merchants, who saw commercial stability stemming from a strong central government, favored the change. But the up-country farmers, jealous of their local rights and fearful of the merchant class, opposed it with all their strength. Hamilton and John Jay worked tirelessly to win them over. James Madison of Virginia helped them out when he joined in their propaganda campaign. The essays they produced are today known as *The Federalist*. They first appeared, hopefully to influence the whole country, immediately after the Constitutional Convention adjourned and before any ratifying convention met. They were widely printed by newspapers. Without them we would know much less about the origins of our government.

By midsummer of 1788, 11 of the 13 states had approved the Constitution. Two held out—but not for long. North Carolina ratified in 1789, and Rhode Island in May, 1790.

The Americans choose up sides

One of the fundamental rights claimed by Americans, from earliest colonial times, was that of dissent. They recognized that there were two sides—at least—to every question and felt that nothing was so healthy as the airing of opposing views. Just as the men who wrote the Constitution debated, so did the American people. Except in some of the smaller states, which were happy to join the Union for its benefits, the debate was long and difficult.

Great issues oblige men to take sides. The contest over ratification divided the nation into those for and those against. Up to this time we had no political parties, but out of this debate there arose the Federalist and Antifederalist groups, which would soon resolve themselves into political organizations with causes of their own. Although the Constitution makers envisaged no such development, the document itself produced a division, and the two-party system was born.

For the moment, however, party politics were submerged. The eyes of the nation turned to the Virginian, George Washington, and for the only time in American history a President was elected without any competition.

AMERICAN PHILOSOPHICAL SOCIETY

THOMAS JEFFERSON

Thomas Jefferson made a great personal contribution to the United States. All his life he had his vision of what this country should be, and he did everything he could to make this vision a reality. He foresaw a United States with a democratic, representative government—one that placed much of the responsibility on the individual and relied little on strong central control. He eloquently set forth his ideas about government in the Declaration of Independence. He continued to advance them in every public post he held. Jefferson also had a vision of his country stretching across the continent. With his encouragement of the Lewis and Clark explorations and his purchase of Louisiana in 1803, he did much to make this dream come true. He took great interest in the kind of education Americans would have, the architecture of the buildings they would erect, and even in what they would grow in their gardens and orchards. He was never a casual bystander. Jefferson was deeply involved in every aspect of American life, and in this involvement lay his greatness.

THOMAS JEFFERSON

JEFFERSON THE RADICAL

MAD TOM in A RAGE

Thomas Jefferson was always a controversial figure. His forcefully democratic ideas as second governor of Virginia (1779–81) were considered radical by many. But Jefferson felt he was only living up to Virginia's revolutionary spirit as expressed on its first state seal above, where Virtue triumphs over the fallen figure of Tyranny bereft of his crown. When Jefferson was inaugurated third President of the United States in 1801, he was no less controversial. The Federalist cartoon at the left supposedly shows Jefferson, referred to as Mad Tom, attempting to pull down the federal government with assistance from the Devil. Such fears stemmed from Jefferson's vigorously expressed sentiments against a strong national government. There was even more headshaking when he bought the huge Louisiana Territory from France, a purchase that more than doubled the size of the United States. New Orleans' historic Place d'Armes (right) was the scene of impressive ceremonies in 1803 as the French tricolor was replaced by the American flag and the United States took possession of what it had bought.

THOMAS JEFFERSON

THE ARCHITECT

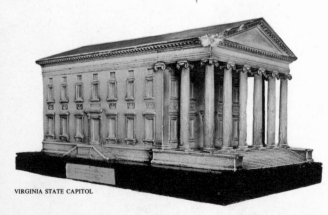

VIRGINIA STATE CAPITOL

Jefferson's energy and talent were boundless. He was a fine architect in the classical tradition. The single building that most influenced his ideas about architecture was the Maison Carree, a Roman ruin in Nimes, France (opposite). He considered it the finest remaining example of classical design. Its lines are mirrored in his own work, especially in the state capitol he designed for Virginia. It still stands in Richmond, and one of the first models of it is seen at the left. Jefferson's last great project was designing the buildings for the University of Virginia in Charlottesville. The 1824 engraving above shows the campus dominated by the great rotunda. Its dome, also typical of Jefferson's style, was inspired by the famous Halle aux Bles in Paris.

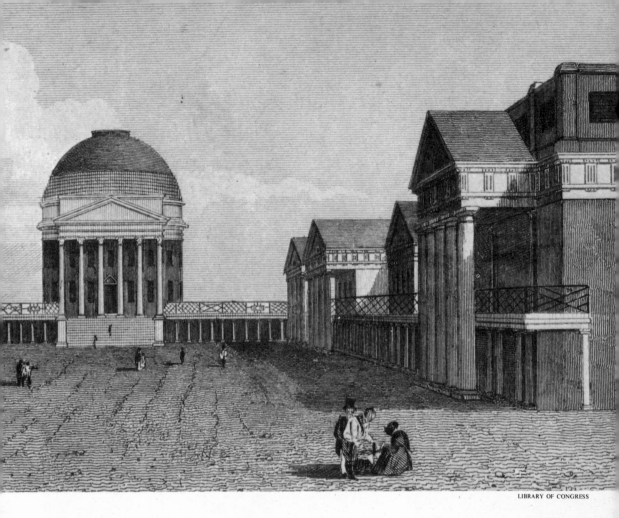

THOMAS JEFFERSON

MR. MAMMOTH

When he was a boy, Thomas Jefferson collected Indian artifacts. As a man, he remained interested in every aspect of natural history—even paleontology, for which his enemies derisively nicknamed him Mr. Mammoth. He was head of the American Philosophical Society, which, in 1801, financed the excavation of the bones of a prehistoric mastodon in New York. Below is the scene painted by Charles Willson Peale, who also belonged to the society. In the portrait opposite, Caleb Boyle painted Jefferson before Virginia's Natural Bridge, which he once owned.

THOMAS JEFFERSON

THE INVENTOR

Jefferson leveled a mountaintop near Charlottesville for Monticello. The cottage (right) where he brought his bride in 1772 was the first part to be built. It was connected to the main house by a semisubterranean series of servants' quarters and kitchens. His law office (left) was connected by a row of stables. At Monticello, Jefferson showed his inventiveness. On his travels he noted anything that made life easier, often adapted it for his own use. A fireplace concealed a dumbwaiter, which brought up wine bottles from the cellar. A quartet stand was devised to hold the music for four musicians. (Jefferson was an enthusiastic violinist.) A polygraph was designed to cut down writing time. As Jefferson wrote with one pen, another made a copy. He wrote more than 25,000 letters.

ter Lacour delin.

A. Doolittle Sc

FEDERAL HALL
The Seat of Congress

CHAPTER 11

WASHINGTON AT THE HELM

In the years since his death, the figure of George Washington—brave, wise, upright—has gradually been turned into a marble statue, as if he had no feelings and never suffered doubt. But turn to his diary for April 16, 1789, as he prepared to assume the first Presidency of the United States under the Constitution:

About 10 o'clock I bade farewell to Mount Vernon, to private life, and to domestic felicity; and with a mind oppressed with more anxious and painful sensations than I have words to express, set out for New York.

The man who had been unanimously chosen for his great office, the man whose calmness, dignity, and strength everyone relied upon to steer the fragile new ship of state, had to borrow money for the trip! Like his country, he had land aplenty, and little cash.

By April 23, he had arrived in New York, which was to serve as the capital for a year until the government would move to Philadelphia. (Gloomy

Washington's first inauguration took place on the balcony of Federal Hall in New York, then the government's capital.

New Yorkers predicted that thereafter their city would become deserted, "a wilderness, peopled with wolves.") As great crowds gathered on April 30 at Federal Hall in Wall Street, Washington made his way to its balcony "accompanied," he said, "by feelings not unlike those of a culprit, who is going to the place of his execution." His voice was low, his manner grave. For the occasion he wore a simple brown suit, woven of 100% American homespun, and only a plain sword to recall the military man—as if to bear witness that this would be a country ruled by civilians. Then he was sworn in by Robert R. Livingston, chancellor of the State of New York, and stepped back inside to address the dignitaries in the Senate chamber.

Much the same group who struggled and fought over the new Constitution at Philadelphia was now on hand in the various branches of the government, united by the desire to make it work, but by little else. There was John Adams, the first Vice-President, founder of a brilliant Massachusetts dynasty, intelligent and honorable, but so pompous in his new dignity that scoffers fell to calling him

This fanciful painting of Washington's arrival in New York for his inauguration presents an image more suitable to King Arthur than life in 18th-century America.

His Rotundity. He was scarcely what we would today call a democrat. "The proposition that the people are the best keepers of their own liberties," he observed, "is not true." There was brilliant John Jay of New York, soon to be the first Chief Justice. His view? "Those who own the country ought to govern it."

And there was one small, dapper, bright-eyed, and handsome man, intensely ambitious—more, perhaps, for his country than himself. This was Washington's former aide and chief author of *The Federalist,* Alexander Hamilton, who had been chosen Secretary of the Treasury. Here are some of his views, for the glimpse they give of how times have changed since 1789:

All communities divide themselves into the few and the many. The first are rich and wellborn, the other the mass of the people. The voice of the people has been said to be the voice of God; and however generally this maxim has been quoted and believed, it is not true in fact. The people are turbulent and changing; they seldom judge or determine right. Give therefore to the first class a distinct, permanent share in the government. They will check the unsteadiness of the second.

But there were other views represented in this remarkable company. There was James Madison of Virginia, advocate of religious liberty, the man who would introduce the Bill of Rights into the Constitution, of which he was the leading author. And there was, above all, that paladin of the rights of man, Thomas Jefferson, the well-bred Virginian who believed in the perfectibility of the "second class" to whom Hamilton referred. In his mind, the ideal society would be an

NEW-YORK HISTORICAL SOCIETY—*New York Daily News*

agrarian republic founded on equality among individual freeholders. He distrusted the cities and the threat of organized finance. He feared powerful industry and a strong central government. It was inevitable that Jefferson would clash with Hamilton, although this was not immediately apparent in the first days of the first administration under the new Constitution.

Unlike any President since his time, Washington did not inherit an already operating machine. Instead, everything had to be created, or done, or even thought of for the first time. There was much to consider as the first Congress began its deliberations. It had to organize itself and provide its own rules. One of the first tasks was the preparation and submission to the various states of the first 10 amendments to the Constitution—the Bill of Rights, urged by Madison. These protections of individual liberty had been demanded by five state ratifying conventions and pledged by Federalist leaders. By December 15, 1791, they had become part of the Constitution.

It was also necessary to provide for the judiciary called for in the charter, including the Supreme Court and the lower courts. As first Chief Justice, Washington appointed a New Yorker, John Jay, and to operate the law enforcement machinery, such as it was, he appointed Edmund Randolph as Attorney General. Departments of War, Treasury, Post Office, and State were also set up, making a cabinet of five. As Secretary of War, Washington appointed his portly and faithful friend, General Henry Knox of Massachusetts; as Secretary of the Treasury, Alexander Hamilton; as Postmaster General, Samuel Osgood, who had commanded a company of minutemen at Lexington; and as Secretary of State, Thomas Jefferson. Although Jefferson had not taken an active part in the work on the Constitution, and was philosophically at odds with Hamilton, Washington trusted him as a friend and neighbor, respected his brilliance and his experience abroad, and felt also that he should strive to

have all viewpoints represented in the administration.

One of the first problems facing the new management was the age-old matter of money. The government was in debt at birth to the extent of about $80,000,000, if foreign, domestic, and state debts were all counted. Daily expenses had begun on March 4, 1789—a provision made by the old Congress in the fall of 1788. Just as soon as the new Representatives took their oaths of office and prepared to function as a body, James Madison introduced the depressing subject. He asked for a temporary tariff law that would raise enough revenue to carry on government functions until a more permanent solution could be found.

Speculators, bootleggers, and finance

A tariff provided only for day-to-day expenses, however. Long-range plans were essential, and Alexander Hamilton now made a series of broad financial proposals aimed at putting the young nation on a more solid footing. Before the federal government's first birthday, he advocated funding the entire foreign and domestic debt into a single obligation. To raise the necessary money, new securities would be offered for sale. His plan was to assume all American obligations, state and federal, from the beginning of the Revolution, at face value. It would still come to $80,000,-000, but the nation's credit abroad would be vastly improved.

The boldness of Hamilton's ap-

Alexander Hamilton, painted here by John Trumbull, was Washington's Secretary of the Treasury from 1789 to 1795, and spokesman for the Federalist Party.

proach aroused great controversy. Many government securities had depreciated heavily—for example, the scrip given to soldiers for their back pay, which was now selling at one-quarter of its face value. At once speculators raced out to the frontier with cash in their pockets, buying up these obligations cheaply from people who did not yet know that they could

soon collect in full. The speculators were, of course, delighted with Hamilton's plan. So also were those states with large debts that would be assumed by the central government. But states whose debts had been paid, or greatly reduced, objected to bailing out their more indigent sisters. Hamilton managed to have his way, but he had to turn to his opponents, Jefferson and Madison, for help. By means of an agreement whereby Virginia was promised Hamilton's support in getting the new capital city located on the Potomac, after 1800, the funding plan won enough Southern votes to squeak by.

Hamilton had just begun to fight. Next he asked for additional revenue to pay the interest on the obligations the government had assumed. He sought it through an excise tax to be laid on such homemade products as distilled liquors. The act passed in March, 1791, and before long the opposition grew so fierce, especially in western Pennsylvania, where tax money was scarce but distilling was a major industry, that Washington was obliged to call out troops in 1794 to put down what has been called the Whiskey Rebellion.

In a country with little cash, Hamilton was far-seeing enough to realize that a credit structure was needed, as it is in any modern state today. Debt —sound debt like federal bonds— is paradoxically the source of credit. Bonds make good paying investments, and bring wealth out of mattresses and strongboxes. Bonds can be borrowed against to provide capital, which starts factories and trade and creates more wealth. Consequently, Hamilton obviously had no intention of paying off his bond issues, which would have deflated the new economy. On the contrary, he sought to provide more credit, and machinery to operate it. Thus he turned to a British model, the Bank of England, and proposed to establish a national bank, supported

by both private and government funds. Jefferson fought this centralization with all his ability, charging that some members of the new government were "driving too fast," and that the Constitution had not mentioned any bank. Madison agreed with him and tried to stem the advance of national power as opposed to that of the states, but to no avail. The bill passed Congress, and President Washington signed it, after asking all his cabinet members their opinion. Hamilton argued most effectively. The Constitution, he said, gave Congress the right to regulate currency and trade, and this delegated power also implied the power to use any legitimate means, not specifically prohibited by the Constitution, to achieve that end. His interpretation is known as the "loose construction" theory of the Constitution, and Jefferson's as the "strict construction."

Hamilton followed his victories with more requests. In December, 1791, he made a report on manufacturing in which he presented a powerful argument for the protection of America's budding industries through tariffs and subsidies. More than a plan for merely fending off foreign competitors by means of a tariff, it antic-

Citizen Genet was sent by the French government in 1793 to get American aid, and although coolly received officially, he was eagerly entertained by the people.

ipated all kinds of improvements, ranging from an increased use of machinery to the encouragement of immigration as a source of labor.

In 1792, an act was passed that strengthened the existing tariffs and generally announced to the world that the government proposed to nurse its industrial fledglings. Hamilton had scored again and had given meaning to Pennsylvania Senator William Maclay's gloomy statement that "Con-gress may go home. Mr. Hamilton is all-powerful, and fails in nothing he attempts."

The crew divides

The Senator's statement was filled with significance. It put into words a sentiment that had already crossed many minds. During the early months of Washington's administration it was increasingly clear that his two assistants, Hamilton and Jefferson, were of

308

divergent opinions in most matters. As the breach widened between them, their supporters, both in and out of Congress, took up the cause, and before the contest was over, America had two political parties, divided on many scores, personal and economic.

Even during the Constitutional Convention at Philadelphia, the merchant class had fought for the kind of government that would offer not only economic stability but specific encouragements to industry. In the Congressional debates over Hamilton's proposals, representatives of this same vocal, intelligent, hard-fighting group banded behind him, overeager to make secure the victory gained at Philadelphia. Because they stressed the need for a strong federal government, as opposed to an association of powerful individual states, they labeled themselves Federalists. President Washington, never formally a party man—indeed, an enemy of "factions"—nevertheless generally supported them more and more because they seemed practical.

Men of the opposition, who at first called themselves Antifederalists and later Democratic-Republicans, did not argue against the notion of national unity, although they wanted less of it, or at least a weaker central government. They agreed that the national debt should be honored, but they felt that Hamilton's plans tipped the scales in favor of merchants, bankers, and speculators. It appeared that the farmer and the planter were to be taxed, excessively they thought, only

to aid bondholders and financiers in the cities. How, they asked, would a national bank assist ordinary countrymen? In short, they charged that the Federalists seemed to be running the government with class legislation.

Jefferson eloquently expressed the view of his followers that the Federalists were warping the Constitution and subverting the rights of the common man. The new government was riven by discord, and Massachusetts Representative Fisher Ames, a sharp-tongued Federalist who soon wearied of hearing his opponents cry "Unconstitutional," dashed off a few angry sentences that perhaps expressed the views of his colleagues: "I scarce know a point which has not produced this cry, not excepting a motion for adjournment. The fishery bill was unconstitutional; it was unconstitutional to receive plans of finance from the Secretary [of the Treasury]; to give bounties; to make the militia worth having; order is unconstitutional; credit is tenfold worse."

Another revolution affects America

If Washington's first administration rang with strife over taxes and finances, his second, to which he was again unanimously elected in 1792, suffered even greater struggles over foreign affairs. The successful Revolution in America had not gone unnoticed in Europe, especially in France, seething with poverty and discontent. Hardly had the new government set itself up in business in 1789 before the European continent was rocked by a revolution in France. The breadth of the Atlantic Ocean did not prevent Americans from taking an active interest; only recently the French had fought against England alongside Washington's army. When the hated Bastille fell in Paris and its worn prisoners streamed into the light, Lafayette sent its key to Washington as a token of revolutionary brotherhood.

As the French Revolution progressed, all followed its course with great interest, but, as was to be expected, there were two sharply divided camps—those who favored the revolutionaries and those who feared them. When the extremist Jacobins came to power, the king and queen were executed, and the guillotine began its long, bloody career under the detested Terror, the conservative Hamilton was appalled; Washington and the other Federalists were inclined to side with him. Jefferson, who had long known the French, took the other point of view. The professed ideals of the revolution were his, and, like many idealists in other times, he could not believe ill of it. He found support from Philip Freneau, editor of an American paper called the *National Gazette*, who used his columns as a mouthpiece for the Antifederalists. And so the two political parties, divided on domestic issues, were now also opposed in foreign affairs.

Differences of opinion over events in France were brought to a head in America by the arrival of a brilliant

"Mad Anthony" Wayne was ordered to avenge the massacre of settlers and soldiers in the Ohio country by Chief Little Turtle.

but unstable young Frenchman named Edmond Charles Genet, called Citizen Genet after the new French egalitarian fashion. He was appointed minister to the United States at the height of the revolutionary turmoil and sent with instructions that looked to embroiling this country in the war France had now declared on Great Britain, Spain, and Holland. Genet landed at Charleston on April 8, 1793, and began a leisurely trip toward Philadelphia. Like the Pied Piper of Hamelin, he fascinated the countryside as he progressed northward. It took him 28 days and an uncounted number of

Wayne routed the Indians in the Battle of Fallen Timbers in Ohio on August 20, 1794. After Little Turtle (center) surrendered, he signed a treaty that ceded southeastern Indiana and southern Ohio for about $9,500 in annuities.

banquets to get there. At the same time, he was abusing his position by trying to organize expeditions against Spanish and British territories, and by commissioning privateers to prey on British ships off American shores.

Meanwhile, Washington became alarmed at the extent of the sympathy for France and on April 22 issued a proclamation of neutrality. He did not use the word itself, but his talk of a "friendly and impartial" course toward the warring powers was enough to make Genet cancel impending testimonial dinners and make haste for Philadelphia, where Washington re-ceived him coolly. Jefferson and Madison, on the other hand, were delighted to meet the Frenchman, and he was so encouraged by their enthusiasm that he wrote home some rather extravagant reports of prospects on this side of the ocean. Presently, however, Jefferson as Secretary of State had to warn Genet to get rid of his privateers and commission no more. The Frenchman promised to comply but secretly armed another, broke a promise to Jefferson, and sent the offender, named *The Little Sarah,* out to sea. The arrogant Genet had hoped to bring America, still officially France's "ally"

311

John Jay, first Chief Justice, wrote extensively on foreign affairs for The Federalist.

under the Treaty of 1778, into the war on her side, but this was not the way to do it.

Hamilton in the meantime had taken the young British minister, George Hammond, under his wing. Between the pressures of the two diplomats, Washington's patience was severely tried. He was relieved when he learned that at last even Jefferson was worried about Genet's conduct. With support from Jefferson, the cabinet asked France to recall her representative in the summer of 1793. Hamilton was pleased also, but his triumph was not complete. Another French minister now arrived, sent by a new ruling faction in Paris, with orders to have

Genet sent home, presumably to be guillotined. Washington refused and allowed Genet to stay in the United States. Jefferson resigned as Secretary of State and was succeeded early in January, 1794, by Edmund Randolph, but Washington was really leaning on Hamilton for advice on foreign affairs, which only grew more complicated.

Jay's controversial treaty

George Washington was anxious to do more than just stay out of war. He wanted to cultivate friendly commercial relations with European nations, particularly England. Despite the Revolution, England remained America's best customer, and the President knew that to prosper, his country must trade. Accordingly, he sent John Jay to London in the spring of 1794 with instructions to negotiate a commercial treaty.

Jay's was a difficult task. His nation was young and unsettled; it had failed to live up to some of its treaty obligations contracted in 1783, and despite Hamilton's efforts, its credit was not yet stable enough to inspire confidence in foreign financial circles.

Yet Jay was supposed to get the British to evacuate the Northwest military posts, and to make them stop encouraging Indian raids on American settlements in the Northwest Territory. He was instructed to persuade Britain to stop seizing American shipping as part of her attempt to blockade the French, and to cease "impressing" American seamen. (So terrible was the life of ordinary seamen in the royal navy of that era that they would desert and ship on American merchant ships whenever they could. In consequence, British men-of-war would search United States ships for their subjects—or supposed subjects—and "impress" them into service.)

After many months of negotiation, Jay came back with a treaty that caused a storm. He had got the British to agree to leave the military posts by 1796, but matters relating to our northern boundary, the settlement of prewar debts, and compensation for British naval seizures were referred to commissions of arbitration, to be settled at a later date. Commercially, America wrung a few concessions out of the British. But nothing was said about impressment or the Indians menacing our frontiers.

When all this was known on this side of the Atlantic, Jay's reputation sank. He had sold out to the British, America's old enemies, and hurt America's friends, the French. He was hanged in effigy, and Hamilton, defending Jay in public, was stoned by a mob. Southern planters and Northern traders were alike unhappy, and even Washington was displeased, for all thought Jay had conceded too much and won too little. But with Hamilton's support, Washington urged the Senate to ratify the treaty as something better than nothing. By a vote of 20 to 10, the exact number needed, the Senators complied, although many of them had been in disagreement with the treaty.

Not long after, George Washington decided to retire. His supporters had persuaded him to run again in 1792, using the argument that his help was needed in getting the new ship of state safely under way. But now affairs appeared to be in much better condition, and the old general turned to writing his farewell address. With the aid of such friends as Alexander Hamilton and James Madison, he set down his last official advice to his countrymen in the fall of 1796. He warned against the danger of the party system and urged his fellow citizens to observe financial good faith and cultivate peace with all countries, suggesting that the nation's remote geographical situation called for a policy of isolation from European affairs.

President John Adams

With Washington in retirement, the Federalists nominated John Adams, and the Democratic-Republicans, with new hope for the Presidency, ran Jefferson against him. Jefferson came within three electoral votes of winning. President Adams, whom Franklin called always honest, often great, and sometimes mad, tried his best to help the Federalists maintain their grip upon the machinery of government, but that young party was already splitting at the seams. Hamilton and his faction did not trust the New Englander. They were further alarmed at his friendship with Jefferson, who had become Vice-President by virtue of coming in second in the election. Blocked at every turn by the Democratic-Republicans in Congress, sometimes ill-served by his friends, and saddled with a poor cabinet, Adams did not enjoy his stay in the White House.

It was in diplomacy that John Adams scored his biggest triumph. Shortly before he came to office, the Jay treaty was put into effect. Although that document professed not to violate any American treaties with the French, it was nevertheless hostile to that nation in spirit. Because the Federalists, particularly Hamilton, were friendly to the British, it was obvious that the treaty would be interpreted in their favor. But reports from Paris made it clear that there would be trouble over the matter.

In fact, when Adams sent Charles Cotesworth Pinckney as United States minister to France in December, 1796, the French refused to receive him. Then, in May, 1797, Adams appointed a three-man commission—Pinckney, John Marshall, and Elbridge Gerry—to obtain a treaty of commerce and friendship with France. Talleyrand, the French foreign minister, delegated three agents (later referred to by the Americans in their dispatches as X, Y, and Z) to meet Adams' representatives, and these three suggested a United States loan to France, along with a bribe of $240,000, as their conditions for a commercial treaty. The

Americans indignantly refused, and Adams brought the matter before Congress, giving it his commission's correspondence concerning X, Y, and Z. Tempers flared. War seemed imminent. George Washington was asked to come out of retirement to lead the army, and a Navy Department was formally established.

Though neither France nor America made a formal declaration of war, an undeclared naval war was begun in November, 1798, when the French captured the American schooner *Retaliation* off Guadeloupe. A number of naval battles ensued in which both French and American ships were captured or destroyed. The Federalists, avowedly anti-French after the radical excesses of the French Revolution, whipped up anti-French feeling to a hysterical point and then enacted some of the most vindictive and undemocratic legislation this country has ever known, all in the name of national security. In June, 1798, they pushed through Congress the Naturalization and Alien Acts. The former extended the requirements of residence before citizenship from five years to 14, and the latter empowered the President to expel undesirable foreigners.

To seal the doom of their enemies, the Federalists also passed a Sedition Act, providing punishment for anyone opposing the execution of the laws or aiding any "riot" or "unlawful assembly," or even anyone who published "any false, scandalous, and malicious writing" which defamed the

Congress or the President. This law sought to silence the Democratic-Republican editors who were sniping at the administration, and sent some of them to jail. Jefferson's followers were so discouraged that one of them suggested to him the dissolution of the Union. However, the answer lay not in breaking up the Union but in a violent protest from the states. Jefferson, the leading advocate of states' rights, drafted a strong resolution against the abuse of central power by the national government; it was formally endorsed by Kentucky lawmakers in 1798. A similar protest, written by James Madison, was shortly approved by the Virginia legislature. The Kentucky and Virginia resolutions held, in general, that the Union was a compact between the states and that as members they had the right to "interpose" when the central government acted in a way not specifically allowed

The monster is the five-headed Directory that ruled France in 1797 and asked the three American representatives for a bribe in the infamous XYZ affair.

in the Constitution—that is, to declare unlawful such legislation as the Alien and Sedition Acts. Although the Supreme Court later maintained that the expulsion of aliens was the business of the central government, these resolutions caused many people to wonder about the nature of the Union, a question that was not settled until the Civil War, if then.

In 1800, when Napoleon Bonaparte had assumed power, French-American hostilities came to an end with the Treaty of Morfontaine, more usually known as the Convention of 1800. This treaty released the United States from its defensive alliance with France and opened the way for increased commerce between the two nations.

The revolution of 1800

Jefferson had no trouble getting his party's nomination in 1800. The party caucus threw its weight behind him and supported glib Aaron Burr of New York, a popular local politician, for the Vice-Presidency. Burr also gained the backing of the New York legislature, which in turn chose the electors. Hamilton thereupon angrily asked for a special session of the legislature to shake loose Burr's grip, but John Jay, who had resigned from the Supreme Court to accept the governorship of New York, politely turned him down.

When the ballots were counted, Jefferson and Burr, both members of the same party, were tied, with 73 votes each. John Adams, running again, had only 65 votes, and his Federalist running mate, C. C. Pinckney, 64. The strange tie between Jefferson and Burr meant that the decision was now up to the House of Representatives. A Federalist House found itself obliged to elect an opposing President, or at least to choose between two members of the other party. The balloting was carried on past mid-February, 1801, with the Representatives in a deadlock. Then Alexander Hamilton made a decision. Swallowing his dislike of Jefferson, he turned against Aaron Burr, who had so recently snatched the New York ballots from the Federalists, and threw his influence to Jefferson. Hamilton hated but respected Jefferson; he hated and distrusted Burr, who remains up to our time a disputed, unloved figure in history.

With Hamilton's statesmanlike action, which would cost him his life on a dueling ground a few years later, the period of Federalist domination came to a close. The Federalists, a good many of whom feared rule by the mob, now shuddered as they waited for the United States to fall into the hands of a Democratic-Republican executive and legislature. With Jefferson, whom they regarded as a wild radical, in power, anarchy would surely be the order of the day. They were to find their fears vastly exaggerated. When the scholarly Virginian took the helm, he demonstrated an axiom that the decades were to bear out: Liberal candidates often make conservative Presidents.

COLLECTION OF IRVING S. OLDS

THE WAR AT SEA

The American Revolution brought political independence to the United States. It took another war to gain recognition for the young country as an equal partner with Great Britain in world commerce. Following the Revolution, the British tried to place as many restrictions on American shipping on the Atlantic and on the Great Lakes as they had in colonial days. The powerful royal navy enforced these rules, seizing and impounding American vessels and crews that broke them. After many such incidents and numerous diplomatic protests, it became apparent that the small United States Navy would have to defend America's rights as a sovereign nation if she wanted to trade where and with whom she pleased. And so the War of 1812 began as a naval conflict. New ships were built and old ships were refitted, and an eager group of young officers was given commands. In two years of fighting, the United States Navy succeeded in doing what before then had seemed impossible: It wrested control of the American shipping lanes from the powerful hands of the British by fighting the royal navy to a standoff.

317

THE BIRTH OF A NAVAL POWER

Commodore Isaac Hull (above) commanded the American warship *Constitution* in her famous battle with the British *Guerriere*. The defeat of the *Guerriere* was the first major sea victory of the war.

The frigate *United States* is shown at the left, flying the flags of the world on her launching day in 1797. It was customary for an important naval vessel to begin her career with this kind of display.

OVERLEAF: The masts of the once-proud *Guerriere* splinter and fall under a withering barrage of cannon fire from the *Constitution*. This fierce duel was fought in the choppy waters off the coast of Halifax, Nova Scotia, on August 19, 1812.

THE MACEDONIAN

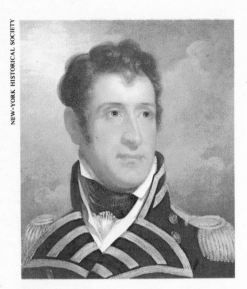

Captain Stephen Decatur first won fame as an American naval officer in 1804, fighting the Barbary pirates. In 1812, he was the captain of the *United States,* on the prowl for British warships.

Both the *United States* and the *Macedonian* had the same basic design as this powerful square-rigged frigate.

On October 25, 1812, Decatur's *United States* (below, right) sighted the British frigate *Macedonian* (below, left), and in a brilliant series of maneuvers she succeeded in delivering a crippling broadside blast to the enemy ship.

1.

3.

THE CONSTITUTION

On December 29, 1812, near Brazil, the *Constitution* struck another blow at British sea power. Here the famous American warship (later known as Old Ironsides) under Commodore Bainbridge defeated the British frigate *Java*. These four aquatints were made from on-the-spot sketches by a Lieutenant Buchanan. The first three trace the destruction of the *Java* under the furious assault of the *Constitution*.

WILLIAM BAINBRIDGE

2.

4.

The diagram at the right records the steps by which the *Constitution* defeated the *Java*, from the first encounter at 2:10 p.m. to the final surrender at 5:25. At the end of the battle the masts of the British ship had been shot away, and she had been leveled almost to the waterline. After the survivors were removed to the *Constitution*, the *Java* was blown up, as shown above in the fourth aquatint.

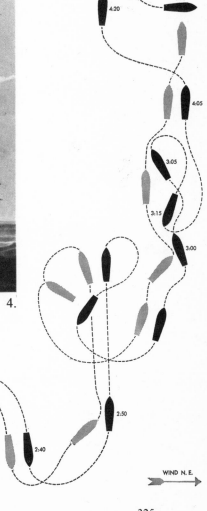

5:25

4:20

4:05

3:05

3:15

3:00

2:50

2:40

TIME—2:10 P.M.

JAVA ------

CONSTITUTION-

WIND N. E.

JAMES LAWRENCE

THE WAR AT SEA

AN AMERICAN DEFEAT

The war at sea was no unbroken series of American victories. One of the worst setbacks for the United States Navy occurred off Boston on June 1, 1813. The British *Shannon,* cruising just beyond the harbor, challenged the American *Chesapeake* to a ship-to-ship duel (left). When the two crashed together, British seamen swarmed off the deck, platforms, and rigging of their ship and onto the *Chesapeake,* where the crews met in open combat. Both sides suffered heavy losses, but the British, fighting savagely and with great experience, were the victors. During the fierce battle aboard the *Chesapeake,* Captain Lawrence (above, left, in white breeches and blue jacket) was mortally wounded. As he lay dying, he gave his final order, which became the rallying cry for the American navy: "Don't give up the ship!"

327

THE WAR AT SEA

ON LAKE ERIE

In 1813, the royal navy controlled the St. Lawrence River and Lake Erie. Supplies for British troops on America's northern borders were brought inland on these waterways. To meet this British menace, a nine-ship fleet was built by the Americans in Erie, Pennsylvania, and placed under the command of a young officer, Oliver Hazard Perry. On September 10, 1813, the American and British fleets met on Lake Erie (above). Perry's flagship, the *Lawrence,* carried a banner with the inspiring last words of Captain Lawrence on it. At a crucial point in the battle, the *Lawrence* was disabled, and Perry calmly took his flag and went aboard the undamaged *Niagara.* In the engraving at the left, of the longboat nearing the new flagship, Perry is standing in the stern of the boat. Victory on Lake Erie came to the Americans after a long, hard battle. When the British had surrendered, Perry sent the now-famous message to Major General Harrison: "We have met the enemy and they are ours."

OLIVER HAZARD PERRY

329

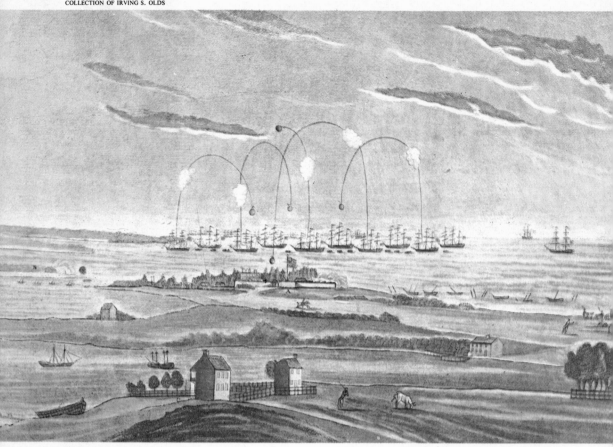

On the night of September 13–14, 1814, a British fleet bombarded American-held Fort McHenry (above, center) just off Chesapeake Bay. British troops were marching on Baltimore, and the fort was one of the few defenses that stood in their way. The little fort repulsed the assault, however, and the British fleet withdrew.

Francis Scott Key was on an American truce ship held by the British until after the bombardment. When he saw his country's flag still flying in the "dawn's early light," he wrote *The Star-Spangled Banner*, which was to become the lyric of our national anthem. Below is his later copy of one of the five verses.

O say can you see, ~~through~~ by the dawn's early light,
What so proudly we hail'd at the twilight's last gleaming,
Whose broad stripes & bright stars through the perilous fight
O'er the ramparts we watch'd, were so gallantly streaming?
And the rocket's red glare, the bomb bursting in air,
Gave proof through the night that our flag was still there,
O say does that star-spangled banner yet wave
O'er the land of the free & the home of the brave?

THE STAR-SPANGLED BANNER

SMITHSONIAN INSTITUTION

All that remains of the star-spangled banner that flew over Fort McHenry during the British bombardment is this battered remnant that now hangs in the Smithsonian Institution in Washington, D.C. This second U.S. flag, 1795–1818, had 15 stars and 15 stripes.

CHAPTER 12

THE REPUBLICAN ERA

When Thomas Jefferson and his party, the Democratic-Republican, replaced the Federalists in 1801, conservative people expected all kinds of trouble, even revolution. But his inaugural address should have somewhat allayed their fears. Trying to smooth out the party bitterness that had erupted while Adams was in office, he said, "We are all Republicans! We are all Federalists!" He wanted the central government to enjoy its full constitutional powers, but he hoped there would be as little federal regulation as possible. Conservatives were relieved to hear him affirm the rights of individual states and to recommend that national expenditures be reduced.

As the new President looked around him, he must have concluded that he needed to move slowly. Washington itself typified the country at large: It was new and primitive, a morass of mud dotted with boardinghouses and shanties. It was inhabited by about 3,000 people, 600 of whom were

Oliver Hazard Perry is shown on his flagship Lawrence *before a banner bearing the words, "Don't give up the ship."*

Negro slaves. The Capitol was unfinished, and so was the President's house. Its roof leaked, the walls were not all plastered, and the floor had already begun to sag as the green lumber shrank. A United States map showed that three new states had joined the 13 original colonies—Vermont, Kentucky, and Tennessee.

On the day before Jefferson took office, the hated sedition laws expired. He had thought them unconstitutional and quickly pardoned those few men still in jail under their provisions. His administration also repealed the liquor taxes that had brought on the Whiskey Rebellion; they had cost as much to enforce as they collected in revenue. Jefferson made another popular move when he appointed Albert Gallatin as Secretary of the Treasury. The Swiss-born financier, a former teacher of French at Harvard College, lived up to the tradition of Alexander Hamilton in many respects. He was a genius with figures; he was determined to balance the budget. And the new Democratic-Republican regime seemed bent upon keeping its promises of economy. Old sailors paled when they learned what was in store

The Capitol around 1800, during the Presidency of John Adams, was only partially completed. It was without the wings and the modern dome it has today.

for them, for Jefferson viewed the naval force as a defensive instrument. He liked the idea already suggested by John Adams that the deep-water navy be reduced in favor of small gunboats suitable for coastal defense.

Yet in spite of Jefferson's determination to avoid a large navy, the United States became involved in a naval war soon after he took office. In a sense, the Tripolitan War was a legacy from the two previous administrations. Both Washington and Adams had continued the practice, begun by the British, of paying tribute to the Barbary States of Algiers, Morocco, Tripoli, and Tunis in order to insure noninterference with American commerce along the North African coast. In May, 1801, the pasha of Tripoli increased his demands for tribute, and when Jefferson hesitated, he declared war on the United States. Commodore Edward Preble was named to lead the American naval forces in the Mediterranean. Although fighting 4,000 miles away from home, and with only the most meager financial support from Congress, the young navy distinguished itself. In June, 1805, a peace treaty favorable to United States interests was signed with Tripoli.

Napoleon makes a sale

To Jefferson, and to the United States, there now came a sudden piece of good fortune. Ever since the Treaty of Paris in 1783, when the western American boundary was set at the Mississippi River, the government had nervously watched as the Spanish occasionally interfered with frontiersmen living in the great valley. In 1762, when French power in North America was breaking up in the last of the French and Indian Wars, Spain had obtained all the vast areas at the foot of the river—and to the west—by the Treaty of Fontainebleau. It was called Louisiana, after the great Louis XIV, but it included much more than Louisiana today. It was an ill-defined area stretching west from the Mississippi, altogether vague in its frontiers.

Then, in 1800, a surprising thing happened. Napoleon Bonaparte, seizing power after France's brief, disastrous experiment with popular government, put pressure on Charles IV of Spain, and that weak monarch traded Spanish Louisiana for a few small thrones and titles in Italy. This trade, made secretly at the Treaty of San Ildefonso, meant that France, at the height of her power, had replaced Great Britain and Spain as the threat to the American West.

Late in 1802, just before the Spanish handed over Louisiana to France, they revoked the right of deposit, and Americans mistakenly assumed that the French were behind the move. New Orleans was once more closed to river traffic, disastrously for Western farmers and traders in those prerailroad days, when everything went down the Mississippi. Angry

Albert Gallatin served as Secretary of the Treasury under Jefferson and Madison.

Kentuckians reached for their rifles, ready to fight the French or anyone else who interfered with their trade. Jefferson wrote at once to Robert Livingston, the American minister to France, with instructions to negotiate to have the port reopened. Then he dispatched James Monroe to help, authorizing him to make an offer for New Orleans and West Florida at $2,000,000, and if need be, to go to $10,000,000.

Events worked for America. Napoleon, vexed because the Spanish had been agonizingly slow about turning over Louisiana to him and smarting under a military defeat sustained while trying to suppress a Negro revolt in Haiti, decided to give up his

335

Robert Livingston, Jefferson's minister to France, negotiated the Louisiana Purchase.

new acquisition. It might, he thought, be taken from him at any time by England, with her sea power and bases in North America. Consequently, to the stunned amazement of Livingston and Monroe, he offered to sell them not just New Orleans but all of the boundless Louisiana Territory. Exceeding their authorization, the two representatives agreed to pay approximately $15,000,000—the price of a few highway cloverleaves today—for a vast and beautiful land that doubled the size of the United States.

The treaty of cession was signed in May, 1803, and approved by the Senate that October. The French flag had barely risen again in New Orleans, to the brief joy of the natives, before it came down, and on December 20, 1803, the Stars and Stripes went up on the old Cabildo, where the Spanish and French councils had sat.

While all this was taking place, Jefferson was already looking to increase our knowledge of the great West—its geography, its peoples, and its resources. Before the purchase was final, he had organized a first transcontinental journey of exploration, headed by Captains Meriwether Lewis and William Clark, brother of the famous George Rogers Clark. On May 14, 1804, they started up the Missouri River on the remarkable trip that would reach the Pacific Ocean in 1805 and bring them safely home a year later.

It was, all in all, one of the greatest bargains in history, better even than the $24 paid for Manhattan by the Dutch—for, payment or not, Europeans would have taken New York, and the same cannot be definitely said of Americans and the West. But the Louisiana Purchase raised thorny questions nevertheless. What of our great principle about the "consent of the governed"? Who had asked the consent of the *habitants* of New Orleans or of the Indian tribes? What about the Constitution and "strict construction"—the principle that the federal government could do nothing not expressly provided by the Constitution? Jefferson searched the sacred document, found little, and became for the moment a "loose constructionist." One must assume, ran

BRITISH POSSESSIONS

Disputed by
the United States
and Great Britain.

OREGON
TERRITORY
Columbia R.
Claimed by Russia,
Spain, the United States,
and Great Britain.

SPANISH POSSESSIONS

OCEAN

Yellowstone R.

LOUISIANA

Platte R.

Missouri R.

Colorado R.

PURCHASE
April 30, 1803

Canadian R.

Red R.

Arkansas R.

Mississippi River

INDIANA TERRITORY

MICHIGAN
TERRITORY

OHIO

Ohio R.

KENTUCKY

TENNESSEE

MISSISSIPPI
TERRITORY

GEORGIA

MAINE

VT.
N.H.
NEW YORK   MASS.
R.I.
CONN.
PENNSYLVANIA
NEW JERSEY
DELAWARE
VIRGINIA

NORTH
CAROLINA
SOUTH
CAROLINA

EAST FLORIDA

ATLANTIC OCEAN

Disputed by Spain
and the United States
after 1803

Rio Grande

Disputed
Territory

GULF OF MEXICO

THE LOUISIANA PURCHASE
Doubled the size of the United States
with the addition of
828,000 square miles of territory.

his argument, that a nation can acquire property, and from that must flow the right to govern it.

Although the President's views prevailed, the Federalists also changed their grounds and bitterly contested Jefferson's actions. Behind the legal talk lay their real fear that agrarian and Western interests in the government would gain from the new lands, and that New England and the trading, commercial Northeast would be overshadowed. New England began to fear a great slave empire spreading into the new territory and dominated by Southerners. Curiously, the Yankees were now talking about the importance of strict construction of the Constitution and states' rights. There

was even some discussion of breaking up the Union and establishing a Northern confederacy.

At this time Aaron Burr, the Vice-President, was running for governor in New York, and New England separatists believed he would join in such a secession, once in office. Alexander Hamilton, who thoroughly disliked Burr, was reported as saying that he was "a dangerous man," too untrustworthy to hold office. Hamilton certainly contributed to his enemy's defeat, and this was too much for Burr, who already had suffered from Hamilton's interference in the contested election of 1800. The Vice-President demanded satisfaction. On the west bank of the Hudson, at Weehawken, New Jersey, one July dawn in 1804, Hamilton, the man who, next to Washington, made the new nation a going concern, took a fatal ball directly through the heart. He had avoided shooting Burr. But the career of Burr, who later became involved in a mysterious, possibly treasonable military adventure in the Southwest, was quite finished.

Virginia dynasty

From the beginning, it seemed that the age of Jefferson would be one of peace and progress. With his architects and engineers he made ambitious plans for the capital city. He promoted immigration, and settlement in the West. Ohio entered the Union in 1803. The Louisiana Purchase elated the President, who began to dream of a great voluntary association of free governments covering the whole Western Hemisphere. His Secretary of the Treasury proclaimed a surplus. His popularity was great.

By Jefferson's second election, in 1804, the system of nominating and electing the President and the Vice-President had been changed; the country did not want another tie like that four years before between two men of the same party. This time, Presidential and Vice-Presidential candidates ran together, as a ticket—in the same way they do today—and the Vice-President was no longer just the candidate with the second highest number of votes. With Burr disgraced, Jefferson had George Clinton of New York

with him on the Democratic-Republican ticket. The failure of the Northern confederacy to break up the Union so weakened the Federalists, who put up C. C. Pinckney and Rufus King, that the Jeffersonians carried every state but Connecticut. It was a smashing victory; the Federalist Party never really recovered. It took another drubbing with the same candidates when, in 1808, Jefferson stepped down —following Washington's precedent of two terms—but ran his hand-picked candidate and fellow-Virginian James Madison, again with George Clinton for Vice-President. Madison swept into office to carry on what was becoming known as the Virginia dynasty.

Sparks from Europe

By then, however, there was only one great issue before America—an issue wished upon it from Europe, for in 1803 the Napoleonic Wars broke out again. The mastery of Europe, and the fate of many ancient states and kingdoms, was at stake. The fact that Napoleon at the outset seemed to be the inheritor and champion of "liberty, equality, and fraternity," the slogan of the French Revolution, blinded many in America to the fact that he was a dictator and cruel tyrant. Anti-British feeling in America harked back to the Revolution and the follies of Lord North's ministry and ignored the fact that England from 1784 until North died in 1806 had (with a brief interruption) been governed by William Pitt, the

Great Commoner, a greater enemy of tyranny than Americans themselves.

Fortunately for free government—in the long view of history—the British also had a fleet. If the Battle of Austerlitz in 1805 gave Bonaparte control of the land, the victory at Trafalgar, although it cost the life of Lord Nelson, gave Britain the seas. In a long struggle lasting until 1815, and at frightful sacrifices to themselves, the British eventually brought Napoleon down. But meanwhile the life of neutrals was difficult; in a death struggle, no one cares much about the rights of bystanders—especially when they are trying to trade with both sides. This, in capsule, is the story of America's relations with Europe between 1804 and 1812, and they culminated in a bloody, unnecessary—yet at moments glorious—final war with England.

In wartime, international law is an early casualty, and American ships suffered abuses at the hands of the belligerents. In only a few years, up through 1807, about 1,500 merchantmen were seized by England and France. The British accused the United States of fraudulent use of its neutral flag, and their attitude became noticeably more hostile. In retaliation, Jefferson, in April, 1806, signed the Non-Importation Act, prohibiting the shipping in of certain goods from England. He vainly hoped the action would cause the British to relax their pressure.

During the same year, Napoleon

About 1800, American sailors were in constant danger of being impressed to serve on British ships. This wood figure representing a sailor of that era was carved as an advertisement to stand before a cigar store.

NEW-YORK HISTORICAL SOCIETY

struck at England with the Berlin Decree, pronouncing all of England under a blockade. The British lashed back in 1807 with the first Order in Council, blockading the entire coast of France. All neutral shipping was warned away from the Continent. Napoleon's answer was the Milan Decree of December, 1807, threatening to confiscate any ship that had entered a British port, paid a tax, or been visited by British officers.

But the grievance that would eventually provoke war was the impressment of American seamen. Thousands were taken off United States ships by the royal navy, and anger was already high when there came what diplomats call an incident.

The Leopard *strikes*

In February, 1807, four British sailors were known to have jumped ship at Norfolk, Virginia; then they had signed on the American frigate *Chesapeake*. Admiral George C. Berkeley, senior British officer on the North American station, ordered his captains to be on the lookout for them. Late in June, the *Chesapeake* headed for the Mediterranean and, before it was more than a few miles off the Virginia Capes, was hailed by H. M. S. *Leopard*. The American ship's decks were still in confusion and her guns were not ready, but the captain was not concerned. He believed that the British ship merely wanted some dispatches delivered to Europe, a common practice in those days. Upon learning that a search was intended, the American ship refused to heave to and was promptly blasted by three broadsides, which killed three men and wounded 18 others. One of the officers of the *Chesapeake* rushed to the galley for a hot coal and with it touched off one of the guns, but to no avail. The *Chesapeake* hove to. Four men were removed from her crew, but only one of them proved to be a British subject; he was later hanged from the yardarm of his own vessel as a deserter. When the *Chesapeake* limped back into port, tattered and torn, the

In 1811, at Tippecanoe Creek, William Henry Harrison defeated the Indian confederacy and earned his famous nickname.

people went wild with anger. British officers ashore were nearly mobbed, and the Virginia militia had to be called out to preserve order. To Jefferson's credit, there was no war. He could have had it for a whisper, but he chose otherwise.

The embargo

Rather than war, Jefferson chose diplomacy, and into the American language came a word that soon drove New Englanders frantic at its sound. The Embargo Act, called the Dambargo by shippers, was designed to bring the European belligerents to their senses by cutting off American supplies. Passed by Congress in De-

340

Tenskwatawa, Tecumseh's one-eyed brother, who was also called The Prophet, was defeated by Harrison at Tippecanoe Creek.

cember, 1807, it provided that no goods would leave our ports for Europe. This was like trying to stop a nosebleed by cutting off the patient's head. Ships rotted at the wharves and commercial life came to a standstill. In the absence of foreign goods, domestic manufactures began to grow. But before long, Americans reverted to breaking a law they did not like, just as they had in colonial days, and a thriving smugglers' trade sprang up between the United States and Canada by way of Lake Champlain and other routes. Across the Atlantic there did come complaints from the British, and signs of unrest that made Jefferson vainly hopeful. But then there

were good crops abroad and eventually, just before he handed the government over to James Madison, Jefferson had to suffer the humiliation of the repeal of the Embargo Act as a failure. Meanwhile, it had so angered New England as to start talk of nullifying what Yankee shippers regarded as a pro-French, anti-British law. In the election of 1808, New England went Federalist.

The Madison administration

Madison was known as Little Jemmy, and indeed he was smaller and, to many, less interesting than his popular, gay, and beautifully dressed wife. But when he became President in March, 1809, he was just as intent upon the preservation of peace as Jefferson. The embargo had just been replaced by the Non-Intercourse Act, under which Americans could trade with anyone but the French or British. If either of them stopped violating our neutral rights, of course, trade would be resumed. At this juncture there appeared on the scene David Erskine, the British minister to Washington, who with his American wife was making a most favorable impression in the capital. Erskine said that the hated Orders in Council of 1807, the basis of most of the contention, would be revoked in June of that

OVERLEAF: *Jefferson, his Embargo Act, and its ill effects are lampooned in this English drawing. Napoleon, hiding behind the chair, is prompting Jefferson.*

341

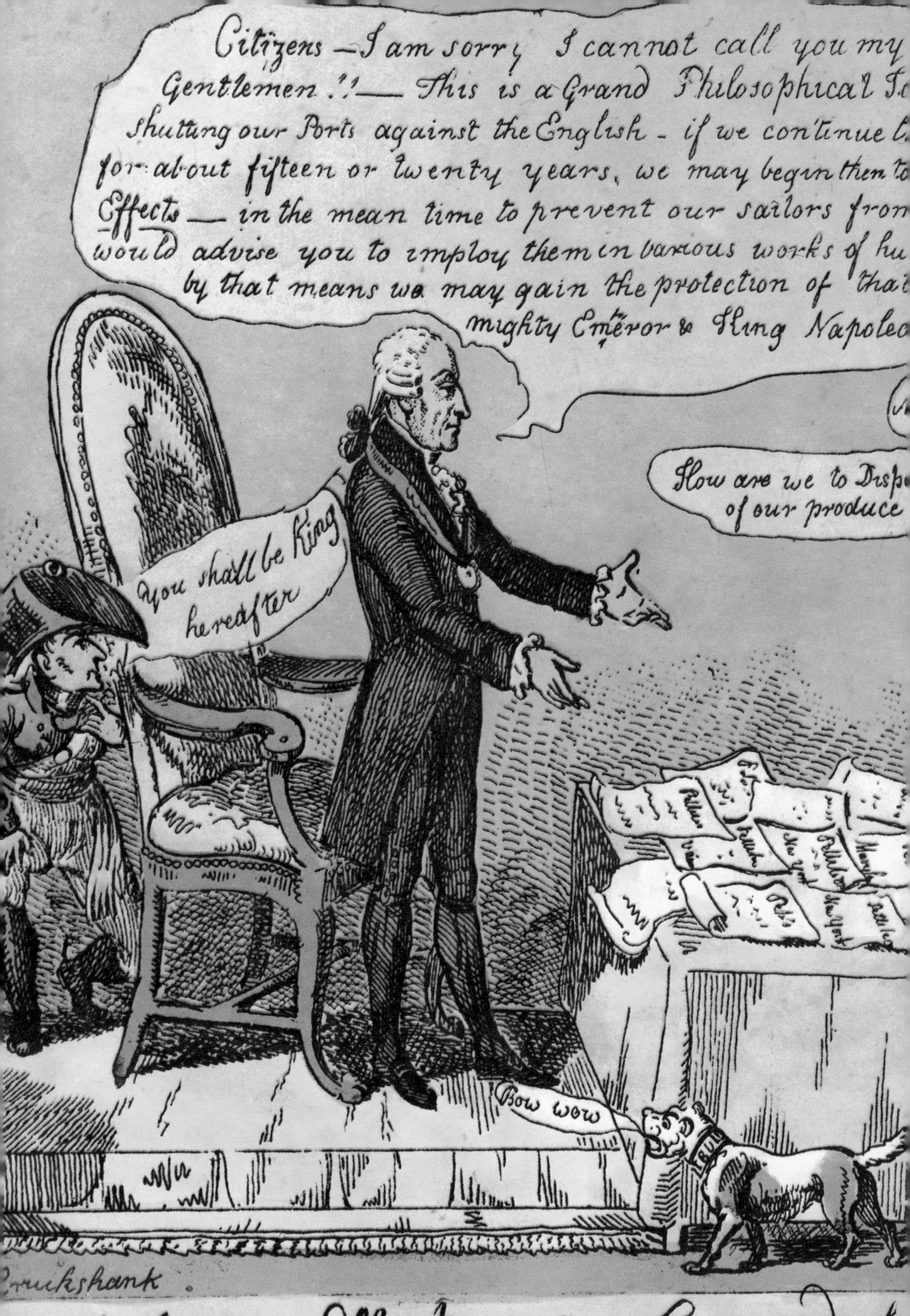

The happy Effects of that Grand Sy

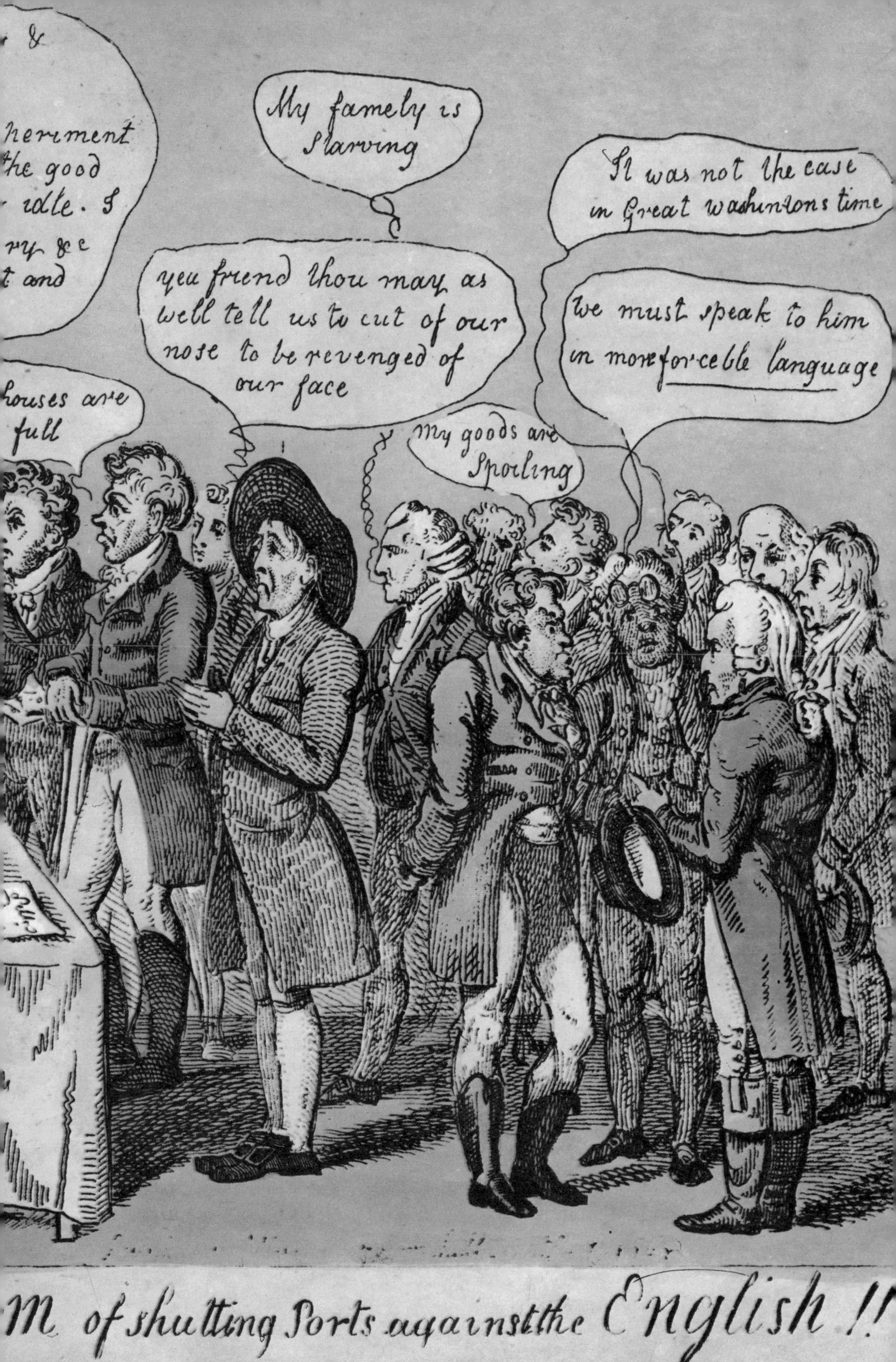

M. of shutting Ports against the English !!

year. Madison, a greenhorn at diplomacy, assumed that the minister had authority for his promise, and legalized trade with Great Britain. Shortly ships were streaming out of American ports bound for England, but Madison was soon disabused of his belief when the British foreign secretary, George Canning, disavowed Erskine's statement. In August, 1809, the President was obliged to reinstate the Non-Intercourse Act against Britain.

Relations with England continued to deteriorate, and the expiration of the Non-Intercourse Act on May 1, 1810, brought no relief. Congress at once supplanted it with a strange piece of legislation called (after its father, Representative Nathaniel Macon of North Carolina) Macon's Bill No. 2. This reopened trade with England and France, but provided that if either country within three months stopped interfering with American shipping, the United States would stop trading with the other. If neither country acted within the time set, non-intercourse would be resumed.

It was the wily Napoleon's turn to fool Madison, and he did so by leading him to believe, quite falsely, that he had cancelled his Berlin and Milan Decrees. Trusting Napoleon's representatives, the President snapped at the bait, warning England in November, 1810, that she would receive no more American goods unless she at once dropped her Orders in Council, too. The British refused for over a year because they knew that Napoleon had not really complied with Madison's demands, and was still seizing our ships, and that in that era of slow communications, we would not find out for many months. On March 2, 1811, Congress cancelled trade with Great Britain.

The war hawks

Tensions were renewed by news from the frontier. Westerners had long complained that the British were paying the Indians for American scalps, and to punish them, General William Henry Harrison, governor of Indiana Territory, moved against the Ohio tribes, which had been organized into a powerful confederacy by the great Shawnee chief, Tecumseh. The meeting took place at the main Indian town at Tippecanoe Creek in November, 1811, when Tecumseh was absent; it gave Harrison both a victory and a nickname that stuck. As the Indians retreated, British arms were found on the field of battle, and the news was quickly transmitted to members of the newly elected Congress of 1811. Many of the new Congressmen came from the West and South, and their reaction was violent. The "buckskin statesmen"—or the war hawks, as John Randolph of Roanoke, the brilliant Virginia eccentric, called these members—were ready to fight. Young Henry Clay of Kentucky, one of the loudest voices, became Speaker of the House, and the Congressional halls now resounded with talk of war.

The war party had its way. "I prefer

the troubled ocean of war . . . with all its calamities . . . to the tranquil and putrescent pool of ignominious peace!" cried Clay.

"Mr. Madison's war"

By June 1, 1812, Madison, who still refused to believe the British when they said Napoleon had deceived him, was driven to declare war. His message recommending it was approved at once by the House, 79 to 49, and after a few days of argument, by the more reluctant Senate, 19 to 13. On June 18, Madison signed the declaration. Thoroughly unprepared for it, the American people were again plunged into conflict with their old adversary. "The blood of the American freemen must flow to cement his [Napoleon's] power," cried the high, angry voice of Randolph.

The War of 1812 is usually regarded as the most unnecessary and unsatis-factory one that America ever fought. It was entered into while news was being brought across the Atlantic that the despised Orders in Council would be suspended. It was bitterly resented by Britons, who felt the United States had stabbed them in the back while they were holding off a menace to civilization. And it concluded with the bloody, pointless Battle of New Orleans, fought two weeks after the peace treaty was signed.

As the military campaigns opened, the Americans carried out their threats and lunged at Canada, but were defeated in each attempt. General William Hull led raw American militia across the border, by way of Detroit, in July, 1812, but soon timidly withdrew. At once Isaac Brock, an excellent British general, rushed troops to Detroit from Niagara. When Brock suggested to Hull that unless he surrendered promptly, the Indian allies

The American attempt to take Canada in 1812 failed because the New York militia refused to support the regulars (in red) who had a toehold at Queenston.

On August 15, 1814, under the command of General Edmund Gaines, 2,000 Americans at Fort Erie repulsed the English attack led by General Gordon Drummond.

of the redcoats might get out of hand in the assault, the dithering defender of the city promptly surrendered without firing a shot. At Fort Dearborn, the present site of Chicago, the garrison evacuated, only to be massacred —men, women, and children—by Potawatomi Indians. Tecumseh threw in his lot with the English. At a single stroke, the American line of defense was thrown back to the Wabash and Ohio Rivers.

An American attempt to take Niagara also failed when the New York militia declined to support the regulars in the battle, causing another withdrawal. Madison's incompetent General Henry Dearborn then tried

an assault against Montreal in November, by way of Lake Champlain, but after marching a few miles, his men balked at crossing the border, on the ground that they had not signed up to fight beyond it. The general turned his troops around and marched back to camp.

The Great Lakes, if they provided a strong barrier against the enemy's land forces, also posed a grave threat from local British fleets. Before the year 1812 was out, it became clear that America must have both a fresh-water and a salt-water navy. During the winter of 1812–13, Captain Oliver Hazard Perry directed the construction from green local timbers of an

American flotilla on Lake Erie. By the summer of 1813, he was on the prowl, searching for enemy craft. He found his prey in the early days of September, at Put-in-Bay, north of the mouth of the Sandusky River in Ohio, and in a bloody three-hour fight won a decisive victory.

Having obtained control of Lake Erie, American troops under General "Tippecanoe" Harrison were able in 1813 to invade Canada, where, at the Battle of the Thames, Chief Tecumseh was slain. This disheartened the Indians and helped secure the Northwest. Other campaigns entered Canada at several points, and in one the capital of Upper Canada, York (now Toronto), was seized and its public buildings burned, a deed that the British remembered when they took Washington. But no real results came of all this fighting. Two attempts to take Montreal fizzled out, and the invasion of Canada was a dismal failure.

Meanwhile, the British had raided and blockaded the coasts until great distress was felt throughout the country. Madison was re-elected with a much-reduced margin over an antiwar party heavily supported by disaffected New England, where active trading with the enemy was going on. The only good news came now and then from the heady exploits of the tiny salt-water navy. At the outset of the war, America had but three major warships, and it was their task to fight off what the British navy could spare from fighting Napoleon. A few days after Hull's surrender at Detroit, his young nephew, Captain Isaac Hull, commanding the *Constitution,* met the *Guerriere* and battered her to bits. In October, the *Wasp* defeated the British vessel *Frolic,* and a week later the *United States* captured the *Macedonian,* taking her to New London as a prize of war.

Disaster in Washington

European events changed the complexion of the war in 1814. The allies entered Paris, forced Napoleon to abdicate, and thus freed thousands of British soldiers for use in Canada. By August, more than 10,000 of the Duke of Wellington's crack troops were assembled at Montreal, ready to crush the Americans once and for all ·in a mighty counteroffensive.

Commanding General Sir George Prevost now moved southward along Lake Champlain. But after a British naval defeat there, he retreated to Canada. To support that badly managed campaign, other British forces landed at Chesapeake Bay and marched on Washington. About 95,-000 American militiamen were summoned to defend their capital, but only 7,000 appeared, commanded by an incompetent general, William Winder, who soon fled from the British regulars, a much smaller force. British officers that evening sat down to a meal prepared for President and Mrs. Madison, who had fled with little but a few papers, some silver, a Stuart portrait of Washington, and

Dolly's parrot. As the Britons dined, their troops burned public buildings throughout the city in retaliation for York.

The invaders now moved on to besiege Baltimore and bombarded Fort McHenry, during which action Francis Scott Key was inspired to produce the words to *The Star-Spangled Banner.* Afterward, the British General Robert Ross, who had dined so well at the White House, was mortally wounded as his forces attempted another landing, and the Chesapeake campaign was called off.

In November, 1814, the British undertook still another thrust. From their base at Jamaica, 7,500 veterans of the Napoleonic campaigns set out through the Gulf of Mexico for an assault on New Orleans. Early in January, General Edward Pakenham sent his British regulars against the 4,500 Americans who defended the city under the bold, brawling General Andrew Jackson, already the winner in a frontier war against the Creek Indians of Alabama. From behind cotton bales piled up as breastworks, the Westerners issued a withering, accurate rifle fire that killed hundreds of enemy soldiers, attacking in close ranks, with flags flying and drums beating the deathly step. No thought of flanking or choosing a better field seems to have assailed the British general's rigid mind. It was Bunker Hill all over again, as if British generals would never learn. Pakenham fell dead; the second in command took

over and was promptly struck down; his replacement also died before the blazing Kentucky long rifles. More than 2,000 disciplined redcoats were killed or wounded in two suicidal attacks before the surviving British withdrew and re-embarked. American losses were 13 killed and 58 wounded. The fact that the battle was fought after peace terms were agreed upon did not lessen the gratification of Americans. They could say they had at last won a great battle, and that did much for national pride, even if no one had won a war. Andrew Jackson, of course, had won a great deal, although this affliction to quiet and conservative people still lay far in the future.

American diplomats had sought peace almost from the outset of the war. On June 12, 1812, a week after entering it but before signing the declaration, Madison asked Secretary of State James Monroe to begin peace negotiations. All he wanted was to have the British give up impressment. During the war, the administration clung to the demand, gradually weakening its stand as the military situation worsened. By June, 1814, American peace commissioners were given permission to stop mentioning it altogether. During that summer, the British suggested a conference at the Belgian town of Ghent, and five American representatives turned up in August to hear their proposals.

The most important aspect of the Peace of Ghent is that it meant a ces-

A view of the Battle of New Orleans from behind the British lines shows the British General Pakenham dying in the arms of an aide after being hit three times.

sation of hostilities. Nothing was said about neutral rights, or blockade, or impressment. Most of the day's burning questions were set aside, to be settled later by commissions. No boundaries were changed; no war reparations were assessed; no privileges were surrendered. All prisoners were returned. Neither side won anything tangible in the nearly three years of fighting. America had lost 1,877 men in action. This was fewer, to be sure, than the number who perished in many single ships in World Wars I and II—but that only reflects the rising horror of scientific war, not the importance of the struggle in which the men of 1812 gave their lives.

Although the War of 1812 might be called a second war for independence, at the end of it America was still economically dependent on Britain. But the war did bring to an end an era in American politics. It was the Federal-

ists in New England who had opposed it, most bitterly in the winter of 1814, at the Hartford Convention, when there had been long and strong talk of secession and a separate peace. But Jackson's victory at New Orleans a year later virtually destroyed the Federalist Party, for it became identified with something close to treason. The Democratic-Republicans, though split into occasional factions, were left as the only party of importance, and for a while partisan feeling subsided.

Americans came out of the war with mixed feelings. During it, they had been hopelessly divided. Now there was a tendency to forget the dissension and look again to the task of building a nation. Putting their international troubles behind them, they faced westward and plunged into domestic affairs, united more than ever before by a struggle that was in most respects a failure.

MAIN TEXT CONTINUES IN VOLUME 5

Charles Willson Peale painted this portrait of himself in the long room of the museum he operated on the second floor of Independence Hall from 1802–26. To the right is the mastodon he dug up, and to the left, above the stuffed birds, portraits of Revolutionary heroes.

The Many-Faceted Mr. Peale

A SPECIAL CONTRIBUTION BY
OLIVER JENSEN

A portrait painter, the founder of a great museum, a scientist and inventor, Charles Willson Peale embodied the spirit of American individualism.

The aide-de-camp strode into the painting room and handed a message to General Washington, who was sitting for his portrait, a miniature for Mrs. Washington. "Ah," he remarked after a mere glance, "Burgoyne is defeated." And then, supremely honoring his young friend the artist, that imperturbable man put aside the dispatch for later study and resumed the pose.

Like Burgoyne, Washington was in good hands. The painter, Charles Willson Peale, a slender Marylander with a long nose and a gentle, curious expression, was well known to him. Peale had taken his likeness at Mount Vernon in 1772, as a colonel of Virginia militia, and again in July, 1776. He had been his fellow campaigner only recently at Trenton, Princeton, and Germantown, a dutiful if not a martial figure who carried both a musket and a palette and who, Washington had noted approvingly while riding by one day, was not above gathering the volunteer company he commanded in a field and cooking them a hot meal. Before his public career was over, Washington was to be painted seven times from life by Peale, more times than by any other artist. It was not always an easy job, as the general noted himself. "At first," he wrote Francis Hopkinson in 1785, "I was as impa-

tient . . . and as restive under the operation as a colt is of the saddle. The next time I submitted very reluctantly, but with less flouncing. Now no dray moves more readily to the thill, than I to the painter's chair."

Peale was much more than the faithful painter of Washington; he was one of the universal men of the 18th century, a man whose talent and interests ran in a hundred different directions—inventor, mechanic, silversmith, watchmaker, millwright, patriot, soldier, politician, and naturalist. His hands could make anything his brain devised, from moving pictures to a new type of bridge. He practiced every branch of the graphic arts—oils, water colors, etching, mezzotint—and he was also a sculptor. He painted most of the heroes of the Revolution from life. He was on friendly, sometimes intimate terms with most of the great figures of his age, with men like Franklin, Lafayette, Benjamin West, Jefferson, Madison, and Thomas Paine. If he had done nothing else, he would deserve to be remembered for founding America's first public art gallery and its first museum of natural history. Although he lived most of his life a few hurried paces ahead of the sheriff, he reared one of the world's happiest and most accomplished families. Under his instruction, dozens of his children and relatives learned to wield the brush. Painting was the cottage industry, and the Peales produced more artists than the Adams family did statesmen, or the Beechers preachers.

Peale himself, however, had no high opinion of his own work at the easel, taking the ac-

cepted contemporary view that "history" was the proper ambition of the painter. To paint great canvases filled with inspiration and allegory and crowded with generals in dress uniform and 18th-century statesmen in togas, in the manner of Benjamin West and John Trumbull, raised the humble "limner" to the heights of art, and in this field he doubted his ability.

Modest in some ways, Peale also loved to shine, sending notices to the papers every time he launched a fresh project. Nevertheless, he was in every way a likable friend, always bustling and enthusiastic, terrified by the prospect

of inactivity, a man who reminds us of Franklin, who respected him, and Jefferson, who so loved and admired him that he sent his grandson to live with the Peales, for his instruction.

In his ideas, Peale was a disciple of the bubbling Age of Reason, a nominal Anglican who was really a Deist, a soldier with a heart so full of affection for all creatures that he became eventually a complete pacifist, a fiery revolutionary so eager to keep on friendly terms with his conservative opponents that he at length forswore politics because of the hard feelings they engendered. Having unwittingly helped

This large portrait of his family was painted by Peale in 1773. Holding a palette and standing in front of an easel, he bends over and watches his brother St. George sketch their mother (far right). His wife Rachel is seated (center), and his brother James smiles at St. George.

expound the unity of science, art, and morality, and the glory of God and Nature.

Peale's own family was not the least extraordinary of his creations, and amused his own contemporaries, especially when he dug into a dictionary of names of classic painters and gave his sons names like Raphaelle, Rembrandt, Rubens, Titian, and Vandyke, artists whose work he knew only by reputation. Female artists were even harder to unearth, and on two of his little girls he inflicted the jaw-breaking names of Angelica Kaufmann and Sophonisba Angusciola. When his attention shifted to science from art, he named two more boys Linnaeus and Franklin, until the second of his three wives put her foot down and demanded a plain Elizabeth.

Altogether, over 40 years, the virile Charles Willson Peale sired 17 children, not counting an 18th who was lost in the childbed death of his second wife. The household included not only his own children but those of his brother and sister, together with various transients—black, white, and American Indian. He took in, as an art student, the orphan (and deaf-mute) son of General Hugh Mercer; he helped a struggling 17-year-old artist with mechanical ideas, named Robert Fulton. There were also brothers and sisters and other relatives, not to mention live bears, birds, and snakes, an elk, and a five-legged cow with two tails—a gift to the museum that provided apparently normal dairy products for the household.

It was a house full of paints and brushes, the clanking of homemade machinery driving away flies, and of music, for nearly everyone sang and played some instrument. Peale could manufacture a fiddle or a xylophone or whatever was required. The place reeked of chemical experiment. Fumes of arsenic, used as a preservative in taxidermy, rose from the kitchen; gunpowder was also manufactured in it; there was a patent "improved fireplace," a

rouse the wartime mob in Philadelphia, he would place himself before the object of its wrath and strive to send the rioters home, and provide carriages for fleeing Tory ladies, and try to save the property, and the feelings, of the other side.

Everything that Peale undertook began in a burst of optimism. Whether it was his apple-paring machine or his polygraph (a device for duplicating letters), his portable steam bath or his new museum, he was certain that it would revolutionize some aspect of life and perpetual oven, and a great deal of work afoot in leather, glass, and porcelain, inasmuch as the head of the family not only made shoes and eyeglasses but also, to the embarrassment of his more socially ambitious children, liked to manufacture false teeth, of a rather modern design, for himself and his friends, and thought seriously in his later years of turning dentist.

This jack-of-all-trades cherished throughout life a number of unorthodox ideas, some of them since justified in the course of history. His medical opinions, for example, were progressive, and, if for no other reason than that he kept most of the bloodletting doctors of the day away from his house, they seemed effective. He ate sparingly, avoided liquor and tobacco (although he made wine on his farm and could not cure his third wife of dipping snuff), and set great store by exercise, proper posture, and a few bowel purgatives that he liked to press on friends. To all his children he was an indulgent, impartial father, modern in his ideas, adamant against the rod, eager to share in their games, striving to interest them in drawing, nature, and what he called "the mechanic arts." He entertained a high opinion, for the times, of the capabilities of women, and saw no reason why his daughters and nieces should not ride the velocipede he devised or why they should not become painters. In the end, several of them succeeded as artists, and one, Sarah Miriam Peale, hung out her shingle as the first American woman painter with a full-scale professional career.

Some of his notions, however, have still not won any general acceptance. He believed that the normal span of a man's life, provided he lived properly and wore loose-fitting garments, should be 200 years (based on the theory that the natural period of maturity in animals is 10 times the length of the immature period). He later revised the figure downward to 112 and seemed, as he reached 86, full of skill and power, well on the road to achieving it. Sharing with the fieriest Whigs a deep faith in the natural rights and equality of all men, he carried the reasoning a step further to the conclusion that there was no such thing as "inborn" talent. Any intelligent man who applied himself, he announced, could learn to be an artist, for example, and, as if to prove his point, set out to teach all his children and nearly all his other relatives the art of painting.

Outrageous and improbable as these theories are, Peale nearly succeeded in proving both of them. He was never so fit, so eupeptic, or so skilled with the brush as in his 70s and 80s. That Peale, who was born in 1741, did not live until 1941 (or at least to 1853, on the revised estimate) indicates, as the old man would probably contend, no fault in the theory, but simply foolishness on his part. He was the first to acknowledge his own shortcomings, to apologize for false accusations, taking newspaper advertisements to make sure his amends reached everyone. In this case, Peale would have admitted, he died because he overstrained his heart, carrying out a feat that would have killed most men half his age. In the middle of the winter of 1827, cold and exhausted, he carried a trunk on his back for a whole mile along a wood path just to save a little time. He was 86, and out courting a prospective fourth wife. Even then, he survived for several months. Death found the old experimenter studying his own failing pulse.

As for the other theory, it is a matter of record that because of Peale's determination, most of the family he instructed in art became good amateurs and at least six of them skilled professionals—among them Rembrandt, Rubens, and Raphaelle. And this was not the end of the talents the elder Peale stirred to life, for there was his placid, devoted younger brother James, who lived with him for years and, from a helper, graduated into a fine artist in his own right, particularly noted for his miniatures. And there were James' son, a fine water colorist, and his three painting daughters—especially Anna Claypoole Peale, who traveled the country with her father and uncle as a miniaturist.

But there was one thing Charles Willson Peale did not know about his heritage: Artistic talent *did* run in the family. His English-born father, Charles Peale, was gifted with the pen; his forte, forgery. He was caught at last with considerable sums embezzled in

Peale's painting of two of his sons was so realistic that Washington politely nodded to it as he passed.

the course of his job at the General Post Office in London, sentenced to hang and then pardoned on condition he emigrate to America. None of this was ever known to the Peales, and the facts were unearthed only in modern times by Peale's zealous biographer and descendant, Charles Coleman Sellers.

In the new country, Peale, Sr., seems to have conducted himself in an exemplary fashion. A gentleman by birth, educated for a time at Cambridge, he taught school among the plantations of Virginia and Maryland, and died when Charles Willson Peale, his eldest son, was nine, leaving his family in poverty. His widow took to needlework for the rich of Annapolis, and reluctantly apprenticed her son to a saddler when he was 13 years old. The boy applied himself and, prospering, bought a cheap watch. It broke and he learned to fix it. He bought a horse and rode into the coun-

try near Annapolis, where he met, at 18, a girl who attracted him—15-year-old Rachel Brewer—and, with no honeyed words or preparation of any sort, blurted out a proposal, allowing her one hour to make up her mind. (Throughout life, he never changed this head-on method of courtship; whatever its demerits, it got results.) When she could not speak a word, he rushed off in vexation, but he returned, and when his apprenticeship was over, they were married, and he set up, on borrowed money, as a saddler himself.

One day Peale journeyed to Norfolk for leather supplies and beheld the first paintings he had ever seen. In the unpublished autobiography that he got together from his diaries many years later, written in an archaic third person, he describes the effect of this experience. The paintings were miserable.

"Had they been better, perhaps they would not have led Peale to the idea of attempting anything in that way, but rather have smothered this faint spark of Genius. . . . The idea of making Pictures having now taken possession of his mind, as soon as he could he begins to try at a Landscape which was much praised by his companions. Next he began a portrait of himself, with a Clock taken to pieces before him, next his Wife's portrait, his Brothers and Sisters. . . . These beginnings were thought a good deal of, and Peale was applyed to by Captain Maybury to draw his and his Lady's portraits, and with some intreaty he at last undertook them, and for which he was to receive 10 pounds, and this gave the first idea to Peale that he possibly might do better by painting than with his other trades. . . ."

With his usual optimism, Peale at once advertised himself as a sign painter in addition to his other endeavors. He went to Philadelphia to buy paints and paid a timid call on a real artist, whom he found, rather inauspiciously, being hustled off by the sheriff for debt. Back home, he offered "one of his best saddles, with its complete furniture" to the artist John Hesselius if, in return, he might be permitted to watch him at work on a picture. Hesselius was agreeable, and even painted half a face so that Peale could fill in the rest.

355

Things did not go well for long with the new family, however. Peale's partner in his saddle business absconded with the cash; then his noisy espousal of the radical side in local politics so irritated his Tory creditors that they descended on him with writs. To avoid imprisonment for debt, Peale fled Annapolis with his wife, and when the sheriff still pursued, he sailed alone in a ship belonging to his brother-in-law to Massachusetts. The exile lasted a year and turned out to be a blessing in disguise. Peale studied for a while with Copley in Boston, and seemed so promising by the time his affairs were put in order and he returned home that a group of 11 wealthy Marylanders, headed by Charles Carroll of Carrollton, raised 81 guineas to send Peale to London to study under the great Benjamin West. Leaving his young wife again, the grateful Peale embarked, in 1766, on a ship which was, to his intense satisfaction, carrying back a cargo of tea that no one had been able to land in the rebellious colonies.

For two years he studied hard under the kindly West, and passed from his primitive colonial methods to a more refined style. In 1769, Peale returned to Maryland, clutching a bundle of painter's supplies and a huge, stilted canvas for his patrons, showing William Pitt in Roman robes orating in the West manner, but the artist himself was arrayed in the colonial clothes, now tattered, he had worn when he left. Patriotically, he would buy nothing in England.

From now on, Peale was to make his living in art, traveling the countryside in Virginia, Maryland, Delaware, and Pennsylvania, painting the gentry in a polished realistic style few of them had ever seen before. In 1776, at the beginning of the war, Peale took his growing family to live permanently in Philadelphia.

Caught up in the excitement of the Revolution, Peale, his friend David Rittenhouse, and his brother-in-law Nathaniel Ramsay made gunpowder at home, and Peale devised a kind of telescopic sight that unfortunately blacked his eye with its recoil the first time he fired the gun on which it was mounted. He joined the militia, and the company quickly elected him lieu-tenant, and later captain. And when Washington, after losing the New York campaign, began to fall back through New Jersey, and Philadelphia filled with alarm at the approach of Cornwallis, Peale raised a company of 81 and took to the field. His brother James and brother-in-law Ramsay were in the regular Continental Army; Peale was distressed to meet them, haggard and worn in defeat. He took a vigorous part in the campaigns around Trenton and Princeton and made the Delaware Crossing; he was on hand for the next campaign when the British, rallying from their defeats in New Jersey, approached and took Philadelphia from the south.

By modern standards, by *any* standards, Peale was a peculiar soldier. Discipline was alien to his nature. His main concern always seemed to be his men, and no body of troops ever had a commander who took their well-being more to heart. He did the foraging, and a lot of the cooking. He doctored his men and, when their boots wore out, procured hides and made them all moccasins by hand with cozy linings of fur. When there was nothing else to do, he painted miniatures of the high officers; he had conceived the idea that he should record, for later exhibition, the great men of the Revolution.

Washington seems to have crossed his path often, and once invited him to dinner. But in riding about searching for clean linen to wear at the occasion, Peale got so far away from headquarters that he failed to show up.

Peale was brave enough and served under fire, but he was not cut to the military measure. Once he came upon some retreating militia and, brandishing his sword as heroes do in romances, tried to rally them. But no one paid any attention, and Peale, having shouted himself hoarse, prudently joined the retreat.

After the tumult of the war, Peale turned to something new. For some time he had given floor space in his home picture gallery to a few old bones, gigantic in size, that had been presented to him as curiosities. One day Ramsay dropped in to see them and bluntly gave it as his opinion that, while a few people might like paintings, things like these bones

Washington's victory at Trenton and Princeton was painted by the elder Peale in 1779. Aided by his brother James, he made more than 20 similar canvases for clients all over the world.

would really bring crowds. Peale agreed enthusiastically.

What began shortly after the Revolution as a picture gallery behind his house at Third and Lombard Streets in Philadelphia, with a few curiosities exhibited here and there, grew into a never-before-equaled collection of birds, animals, and reptiles, arranged according to the classical order of Linnaeus, handsomely mounted and stuffed by Peale and his family. Many he had caught himself, with gun and bag. Others were contributed by his friends. (Franklin once sent him the corpse of his French angora cat and Washington some dead pheasants. Jefferson shipped him specimens brought back by the Lewis and Clark expedition.) That other animal, man (anticipating Darwin, Peale was sure of some relationship with monkeys), was represented not only by Peale's rows of portraits but by elaborate life-size waxworks of the various races.

Peale took his duties seriously. He placed all his specimens in natural surroundings, part stage set, part painted backdrop. (A hundred years ahead of his time, he had invented the "habitat" group.) There were, in addition, displays of minerals, of insects, and all branches of natural history; 100,000 items altogether, including the trigger finger of an executed murderer. A live eagle screamed in the rafters; the first complete mastodon skeleton ever assembled stood in a place of honor. Peale, who thought it was a mammoth, had dug it up.

As the museum grew, it moved to Philosophical Hall and finally into the second story of Independence Hall, which cost Peale $400 a year rent but lent a quasi-official air to the enterprise. It was a lively, bustling place, with a daughter playing a big organ, the sons lecturing, and occasional exhibits of such strange things as "moving pictures," an elaborate animated mechanical device of Peale's. Anticipating Hollywood by some hundred years, he had contrived a group of moving stage sets, complete with music and sound effects. Night fell over Market Street; Satan's Palace, as described by Milton, gave off a fiery pageantry; the *Bonhomme Richard* approached the *Serapis* and took her captive. For this last production, wooden waves moved mechanically in the foreground while transparent moving curtains passed "clouds" over the scene. Holes appeared in the sails and, as night fell, the American ship sank and the victors sailed off. Mrs. Peale took tickets.

There was an air of fun and excitement that one never finds in the respectable hush of modern museums. Once a dinner was given inside the huge skeleton of the mastodon and toasts were drunk to peace, progress, and so forth—Peale, a teetotaler, abstaining.

Unaccustomed as they were to solvency, the Peales basked for years in comparative wealth as the museum prospered. Peale, stunned at first by Rachel's death in 1790, went courting again the next year, married a New Yorker named Betsy de Peyster, and added to his family. He supported the improvident Raphaelle, and sent Rembrandt and Rubens abroad. Widowed again in 1804, he presently married his third wife, the Quaker Hannah Moore. About 1809 he bought a country place he called Farm Persevere, and later Belfield, and here he undertook, for a time, scientific agriculture.

Eventually, Peale returned to Philadelphia, his museum, and his first love, painting. He traveled to Washington with his pretty and skillful nieces, painting celebrities and dining at the White House. Always he seemed to catch his subjects in a moment of lively awareness. And although he still lacked confidence in his ability to paint "history," he was recording it at every stroke.

Jack-of-all-trades and master of several, Charles Willson Peale was in many respects a boy who never grew up, as several of his contemporaries noted: He was a pacifist who never lost his love of bright uniforms, an idealist with the manner of a promoter, a moralist who loved a good time. Curious, noisy, and upright, he came as close as any man could to embodying the American spirit in all the joy and optimism of its youth.

Oliver Jensen, the editor of American Heritage Magazine, *is the author of many articles on American history and two books—*Carrier War *and* The Revolt of the American Woman.

FOR FURTHER READING

Abernethy, Thomas P. *The Burr Conspiracy.* New York: Oxford University Press, 1954. The most objective and scholarly account of a controversial figure.

Adams, Henry. *History of the United States of America During the Administration of Jefferson and Madison.* 9 volumes. New York: Scribner, 1889–91. These volumes can be studied separately. Although written in the 19th century, they remain the major work on the period and an example of some fine historical prose. *The War of 1812,* ed. Major H. A. DeWeerd. Washington: The Infantry Journal, 1944. Chapters from the above nine volumes that thoroughly cover the war years. *The Formative Years,* Herbert Agar, Boston: Houghton Mifflin, 1947. A two-volume abridgement of the nine-volume Adams work.

Bailey, Thomas A. *A Diplomatic History of the American People.* 6th edition. New York: Appleton-Century-Crofts, 1958. An unusually readable book with sections applicable to this volume.

Beard, Charles. *Economic Origins of Jeffersonian Democracy.* New York: Macmillan, 1952. A study of the economic foundations of democracy as interpreted by Jefferson.

Beirne, F. F. *The War of 1812.* New York: E. P. Dutton, 1949. The war and the events leading up to it.

Bowers, Claude G. *Jefferson and Hamilton.* Boston: Houghton Mifflin, 1925. This study of the two controversial figures tends to favor Jefferson.

Brant, Irving. *James Madison.* 6 volumes. Indianapolis: Bobbs-Merrill, 1941–61. Still not completed, this is the comprehensive work on Madison.

Chinard, Gilbert. *Thomas Jefferson.* Ann Arbor: University of Michigan Press, 1929. One of several good books on Jefferson.

Jefferson, Thomas. *The Life and Selected Writings of Jefferson,* ed. Adrienne Koch and William Peden. New York: Random House, The Modern Library, 1944. A short biography and a good collection of Jefferson's writings.

Jensen, Merrill. *The New Nation: A History of the United States During the Confederation, 1781–89.* New York: Knopf, 1950. A concise and lucid narrative of the events of greatest national concern.

Kurtz, Stephen G. *The Presidency of John Adams.* Philadelphia: University of Pennsylvania Press, 1957. In the author's view, the Adams administration is not the negative hiatus that some historians have considered it.

Malone, Dumas. *Jefferson and His Times.* 3 volumes. Boston: Little, Brown, 1948, 1951, 1962. The major study of Jefferson, well written and perceptive.

Miller, John C. *The Federalist Era, 1789–1801.* New York: Harper, 1960.

Monaghan, Frank. *John Jay, Defender of Liberty.* Indianapolis: Bobbs-Merrill, 1935. A fine biography that also covers the main elements of Jay's and Pinckney's treaties.

Padover, S. K. *Jefferson: A Great American's Life and Ideas.* New York: Harcourt, Brace, 1942. Another good one-volume study of Jefferson.

Pratt, Julius W. *Expansionists of 1812.* New York: Macmillan, 1925. Gives the background of the war and the problems of neutrality.

Tucker, Glenn. *Poltroons and Patriots: A Popular Account of the War of 1812.* 2 volumes. Indianapolis: Bobbs-Merrill, 1954. A well-written and colorful account, with much material drawn from newspapers.

THE AMERICAN HERITAGE NEW ILLUSTRATED HISTORY OF THE UNITED STATES

PUBLISHED BY DELL PUBLISHING CO., INC.

George T. Delacorte, Jr., *Publisher*   Helen Meyer, *President*
William F. Callahan, Jr., *Executive Vice-President*

Walter B. J. Mitchell, Jr., *Project Director;* Ross Claiborne, *Editorial Consultant;* William O'Gorman, *Editorial Assistant;* John Van Zwienen, *Art Consultant;* Rosalie Barrow, *Production Manager*

CREATED AND DESIGNED BY THE EDITORS OF AMERICAN HERITAGE MAGAZINE

James Parton, *Publisher;* Joseph J. Thorndike, Jr., *Editorial Director;* Bruce Catton, *Senior Editor;*
Oliver Jensen, *Editor;* Richard M. Ketchum, *Editor, Book Division;* Irwin Glusker, *Art Director*

ROBERT R. ENDICOTT, *Project Editor-in-Chief*

James Kraft, *Assistant Editor;* Nina Page, Evelyn H. Register, Lynn Marett, *Editorial Assistants;*
Lina Mainiero, *Copy Editor;* Murray Belsky, *Art Director;* Eleanor A. Dye, *Designer;* John Conley, *Assistant*